Praise for *The $64 Tomato*

"Engaging, well paced and informative."
—*The New York Times Book Review*

"A wry memoir in which every reader who's spent more to grow a plant than he could purchase it for at the supermarket will recognize his own success, failures and foibles."
—*San Francisco Chronicle*

"Both an inspiration and a cautionary tale for anyone who has ever looked at a tomato and thought, *I could grow that!*"
—*Life* magazine

"A genuinely humorous book that debunks the American dream not in the familiar economic sense but in its rural incarnation. It is a paean to the homesteader who never gets written about, the pioneer whom all of us could have been in another life."
—*The Washington Post Book World*

"Money, sex, and aging. *That's* real gardening!"
—*The New York Observer*

"Engaging, funny, and down-to-earth."
—*Entertainment Weekly*

"William Alexander transcends the inevitable failures with bushel baskets of self-deprecating wit. As a bonus, bits of practical information are scattered as freely as seeds among the hilarious anecdotes."
—*The Charlotte Observer*

"You don't have to be a gardener to enjoy and learn from William Alexander's derring-do. You don't have to know a shuffle hoe from a reel mower to laugh out loud."

—*The State* (SC)

"A quick read full of fun and foibles. And because the adversaries are worthy opponents, combat is fair."

—*The Seattle Times*

"A rollicking read." —*New York Newsday*

"Reminiscent of the movie comedy *Mr. Blandings Builds His Dream House.* . . . Enjoyable, thought-provoking."

—*The National Gardener*

"Often hilarious. . . . Will strike a universal chord."

—*The Dallas Morning News*

"A witty memoir proving that Mother Earth can't be controlled, especially when beetles, worms and grubs come out to play." —*The Economist*

"Readers who have decided to try 'growing a vegetable or two' will, instead, laugh uproariously at author William Alexander's tales of squirrel armies, organic growing and a woodchuck that would make Dr. Frankenstein proud."

—*The Louisville Courier-Journal*

"Recounts with wry humor and dead-on insights [Alexander's] joys, woes, epiphanies, and philosophies. . . . [This] book will strike a chord (and hit a few nerves) with anyone who dreams of orderly rows of ripening veggies and eating a tomato fresh off the vine." —*Garden Design* magazine

"[A] hilarious horticultural memoir. . . . Even if you never plant a seed in your life, *The $64 Tomato* will give you a healthy appreciation of the fact that we will never be able to completely control Mother Earth."

—*The St. Petersburg Times*

"Alexander's account is a delightful guide to achieving gardening bliss. . . . Humor, it turns out, is essential, and Alexander has a large store of it; it infuses his story from start to finish."

—*The Minneapolis Star Tribune*

"The subtitle applies to just about everybody who ever stuck a spade into soil. So what makes Alexander different? He can write about his mistakes and successes—and there are plenty of both—in a funny, self-deprecating way."

—*Richmond Times-Dispatch*

"For a breezy summer read or a break from trying to get in those peppers after all the rain we've had, *The $64 Tomato* will leave you laughing and understanding why Adam and Eve might think Eden wasn't such a great place after all."

—*The Rutland (VT) Herald*

"An amusing romp through one man's innocent little dream."

—*CS* (Chicago)

"[Alexander] admits to his madness with a wry and rueful sense of humor . . . [and] treats us to an often rib-tickling tale of his misadventures." —*The Raleigh News & Observer*

"This enjoyable book, laced with humor and Alexander's garden philosophy, is highly recommended."

—*Library Journal*

THE
$64
TOMATO

William Alexander

ALGONQUIN BOOKS
OF CHAPEL HILL
2007

Author's Note:
While the people and events described in the following pages are real,
some names have been changed for the sake of privacy.

Published by
ALGONQUIN BOOKS OF CHAPEL HILL
Post Office Box 2225
Chapel Hill, NC 27515-2225

a division of
WORKMAN PUBLISHING
225 Varick Street
New York, New York 10014

Library of Congress Cataloging-in-Publication Data
Alexander, William, 1953–
    The $64 tomato / William Alexander.
      p. cm.
    ISBN-13: 978-1-56512-503-2 (HC)
    1. Vegetable gardening—Hudson River Valley Region (N.Y. and
N.J.)—Anecdotes. 2. Gardeners—Hudson River Valley Region
(N.Y. and N.J.)—Anecdotes. 3. Alexander, William, 1953–
I. Title: Sixty-four dollar tomato. II. Title.
SB320.7.N7A44 2006
635.09747'3— dc22   2005053790

ISBN-13: 978-1-56512-557-5 (PB)

10 9 8 7 6 5 4

For Anne, Zach, and Katie

And to the memory of my father, William Alexander

I will go to the garden.
I will be a romantic. I will sell
myself in hell,
in heaven also I will be.

—Robert Creeley, "The Door"

There's a fine line between gardening
and madness.

—Cliff Clavin in *Cheers*

CONTENTS

Gentleman Farmer

"Why can't Dad be more like other dads?" Katie asked my wife recently. "All my friends' dads spend Sundays watching football and drinking beer." Then for good measure she added, "I wish we had a normal family."

I was flabbergasted when I heard this. This is a thirteen-year-old's ideal of a father? Belching beer in front of the TV on a Sunday afternoon? I realize that most teenage girls think their families are weird (and their friends' families cool), but still I was a little hurt. While this conversation was taking place, I was in the garden, of course, even though it was December. The first hard freeze of the season was coming in overnight, and I needed to harvest the remaining leeks. Later, while the Jets were blowing a close one, I was in the kitchen, making steaming leek-potato soup that Katie positively swooned over at dinner. And she wanted to trade me in for a beer-drinking couch potato?

Granted, I have my obsessions and eccentricities, the garden being the most obvious, and maybe I'm not a *typical* dad, but I'm certainly *normal*. I decided to visit Zach's bedroom for a reality check from a levelheaded seventeen-year-old.

"Zach, you'd say I'm a normal dad and we're a normal family, wouldn't you?"

"Ah-ha-ha-ha-ha-ha . . ." He nearly fell out of his chair, where he might have vanished for days beneath a deep pile of unwashed laundry, sweatshirts, textbooks, magazines, a trombone and a euphonium, and two guitars.

"I'll take that as a no?"

"You've got to be kidding," Zach said, turning to face me directly. Zach has mastered the teenage art of subtly turning the tables on parent-child roles and making me feel the child, sheepish and a little embarrassed as he assumes the role of wise parent. "Nothing is normal about this family," he lectured, not smiling.

I've long known that I'm a little short on self-awareness, but this gap between my very own kids' perception of our family life and mine was shocking nonetheless.

"In what ways, Zach? It feels pretty normal to me."

"Dad, just look around," Zach said, becoming exasperated with my denseness. "Take this house, for one. And you just came in from the garden. In freakin' *December.*"

"How was that leek soup tonight?"

"And you *cook.*"

"It was good, wasn't it? I think the leeks are sweeter late in the year."

Zach spun his chair back to his computer, sighing and shaking his head. "December," I heard him mutter under his breath.

Whore in the Bedroom, Horticulturist in the Garden

Nature, Mr. Allnutt,
is what we are put in this world to rise above.
—Katharine Hepburn to Humphrey Bogart
in *The African Queen*

Bridget arrived for her interview late, breathless, and blond. As we drank herbal tea around the kitchen table, she dug deep into a leather portfolio, emerging with glossy photographs of gardens she had designed for previous clients. Anne ooh-aahed over the photographs, which looked like rather ordinary gardens to me, but to be fair, I was only seeing them peripherally. My eyes were riveted on the hands holding the photographs. Delicate, lightly freckled hands with dirty—filthy—fingernails. Real gardener's fingernails. The effect was startling, at once repulsive and erotic. The phrase *whore in the bedroom, horticulturist in the garden* popped into my head. I tried to blink it away. When I finally looked up, Bridget smiled and squinted her crinkly green eyes at me.

A winkless wink. Had I been caught ogling her dirty hands?

After reviewing her credentials and our project, we strolled through the property, Bridget and I falling into lockstep as Anne trailed slightly behind. Passing various anonymous plants and flowers, Bridget would point to what was to me some nameless weedy shrub and exclaim in a breathless whisper something like, "Ah, a beautiful *Maximus clitoris*." She knew *all* the botanical names, the Latin rolling off her tongue like steamy profanity in the heat of passion.

We hired Bridget on the spot, without interviewing anyone else. It seems she'd made an impression on Anne as well.

"Did you notice her beautiful teeth?" Anne sighed as Bridget drove off in her battered Toyota, vanishing in a cloud of smoke and noise.

Beautiful *teeth*? Who were we talking about, Seabiscuit? My wife, a physician, tends to be a little clinical at times. Sometimes I catch her taking my pulse or listening to my heart murmur while *I* think we're making love. So the fact that she would sit across from a beautiful woman and mainly notice her teeth should not have surprised me. In fact, Anne is fascinated with, and jealous of, anyone with better teeth than she, which is to say just about anyone born after about 1970.

"Her teeth? Not really," I said, being more interested in my burgeoning dirty-fingernail fetish.

We hired Bridget even though she had never designed a vegetable garden. Who has, after all? People hire landscape architects to design entire landscapes, or patio and pool plantings, or civic gardens. Who hires a professional to figure out where to put the tomatoes? You put down a few railroad ties and throw down some seeds, right? Not us.

After two years of staring at "the baseball field," the elongated, sloping piece of land in a hollow between our kitchen and the neighbors' driveway, and after hours of studying garden-design books, we still hadn't a clue how to proceed. We wanted something more than the usual boring rectangular beds. We wanted a little pizzazz with our parsley. And it was, to be sure, a challenging space. Bordered on our neighbors' side by a railroad-tie retaining wall and on the opposite side by our ninety-year-old stone wall, the garden was oddly below grade and, after a rain, held water like a huge sponge. Furthermore, it sloped about fifteen feet along its seventy-five-foot length, so some type of terracing seemed inevitable. We needed professional help.

The fact that we even had a suitable plot for a garden had come as a bit of a surprise. We had nicknamed the area "the baseball field" because both before and after we moved into our house, the neighborhood kids used it daily for baseball. Not our kids, of course. Katie was still a toddler, and Zach—well, the most useful thing Zach had ever done with a baseball bat was to use it at age five to reach the screen door latch, locking me out of the house while I was waiting on the porch with my glove and ball. He wanted to stay inside and read, not play baseball with his dad.

So the four of us watched from afar as the kids next door played spirited baseball games in the field. We assumed the land belonged to our next-door neighbors Larry and Claire, whose two sons spent most of their summer afternoons on it. We watched curiously that first summer as the games became difficult when the unmowed grass grew ankle high, then stopped altogether when the grass reached knee height. One day I finally flagged Larry down while he was mowing the rest of his yard and asked why he'd stopped mowing the field. He looked at me as if I were an idiot and said, "Because it's yours," gave a tug on his mower, and was off.

Ours? My first, instinctive reaction was, "Wow, I've got more land than I thought! What a deal!" I ran inside to tell Anne. She was, well, unimpressed. Or more accurately, not interested. Clearly the territorial gene resides on the Y chromosome. But even my landowner's euphoria quickly faded to a more sobering, "Jesus, this worthless patch of lawn is going to add another half hour of mowing every week." Not to mention that it was now midsummer and the grass had grown to a height of two feet. My third reaction—if you can call a thought that takes several years to arrive a reaction—was, "What a great spot for a kitchen garden." Not a mere patch for a few tomatoes and baseball-bat-size zucchini (we had already done that), but a real, landscaped, eat-your-heart-out-Monet, garden-magazine-quality garden—only we would grow mainly vegetables instead of flowers in it.

Bridget, she of the Scandinavian green eyes and strawberry blond hair, with her perfect teeth and botanical Latin, would design it. Her husband, a landscaper who specialized in garden construction, would build it. One contractor, no hassle. That's the way we like it.

Bridget had promised us a preliminary plan in two weeks. As it was just early summer, we had plenty of time. Our goal was to have construction started by Labor Day; that would allow plenty of time to complete the project before the autumn rains turned our yard into a quagmire of slick yellow clay. We really wanted the garden completed by fall, because we were eager to get early potatoes, peas, and spinach planted the following March. If construction was delayed till spring, who knew when it would be completed, and we would lose a half year of crops. Bridget readily agreed that Labor Day was no problem.

Two weeks came and went, then three. No plan. Two months passed. Finally Bridget called. She had the plans, behind schedule, she acknowledged, but worth waiting for. A few days later, Bridget arrived, still late, breathless, and blond. And smelling of the earth, of a fresh potato patch. She unrolled a large, professional-looking blueprint onto the kitchen table, smoothing it out under her dirty fingernails. It was a lovely work of art, with carefully drawn circles for shrubs, and smaller circles for plants, and little curly things for flowers, with (of course) Latin names indicated for everything. The content, however, was not what I had envisioned. Her design was essentially rows of rectangular beds, separated by two grass paths running up the middle and transversely across the garden. There were some nice touches: where the paths intersected, she had put in stone circles with birdbaths or ornaments, and she had a nice stone staircase descending to the sunken garden. It was a perfectly fine garden, it was just a little . . . I struggled for a word, just the right word, as Bridget nervously studied my face. "Cartesian," I said.

Bridget blinked. "Cartesian?"

I looked to Anne for help. She pretended not to know me.

"You know," I said. "Rectangular. Planar. I guess we had something more rambling in mind."

Bridget looked at the plan and thought for a minute, and this is what she must have said to herself: "My husband is going to use Big Machinery to shape and terrace the land; therefore the terraces have to be perpendicular. Irregularly shaped terraces would require him to build them by hand, which he is not about to do at any price."

Obviously, she couldn't say *that* to a client. Here instead is the translation she supplied to the naive and gullible homeowner.

"The problem is, Bill"—it was strange, tingly, and totally convincing to hear her say my name—"you have to terrace it to deal with the slope, and terraces have to be rectangular."

Oh. Well, that shows how much I know. Of course, terraces have to be rectangular. (It would be some years before I realized the blatant untruth of that statement.) Okay, so much for winding, rambling paths. Rectangular is fine. I moved my attention to the broad, grassy paths. "I don't know that I like the idea of having to *mow* my garden. Can we put something else in here?"

Bridget crinkled her green eyes at me. "But, *Bill,* the grass paths will look so *grand,*" she insisted. "So stately. And the mowing is nothing. Two swipes with the mower. You think about it; I know you'll want the grass." I looked to Anne for guidance, but she was gazing at Bridget.

The garden architect flashed her pearlies in Anne's direction. Anne, I think involuntarily, smiled back. What kind of spell had this Valkyrie cast over us?

Okay, rectangular and grassy. Sounds good to me. And she does have all those beautiful architectural symbols and Latin names, and the great teeth. We wrote out a check and agreed we would see her husband around Labor Day.

As Labor Day approached, Anne and I were flush with excitement. We had signed a contract, made a down payment for the construction phase, and spent our idle minutes running our fingers over the smooth blueprints and poring over seed catalogs. One moonless night in August, we grabbed some blankets and lay on our backs in the tall grass in the garden-to-be, touching hands, looking at the constellations, discussing what to plant. We were going to have a two-thousand-square-foot garden next year! To a couple of former city dwellers, this seemed like a small farm. No more agonizing decisions over whether to plant squash or lettuce. We could plant *everything*. I fancied myself a small farmer, self-sufficient in vegetables for at least several months of the year, and longer for storage crops like potatoes and winter squash. With the occasional shooting star shamelessly egging us on, Anne topped my ambitions with her romantic dreams of canning, making the garden's bounty last *twelve* months of the year. I responded with homemade sun-dried tomatoes, tasting of sunshine and acidic sweetness.

"Fresh blueberries," Anne moaned, "that turn your lips blue."

"Cherry tomatoes," I countered. "Popped whole into your mouth."

Before long we were rolling in the summer grass, our way of saying farewell to the baseball field with its little vegetable patch and welcoming the kitchen garden.

With these tantalizing visions dangling before us, we didn't mind sacrificing the last few late tomatoes of the year, ripping out the plants and disassembling the beds in anticipation of Big Machinery that would be arriving any day.

Labor Day arrived. No Big Machinery. I called Bridget to try to get a start date.

"George is held up on a job on Long Island," she explained. "He spends every summer working on an estate, and the job's running long this year. But we'll definitely be starting by Columbus Day."

Long Island? That's a hundred miles away. This guy gets around.

"You don't say, Bridget. I'm from Long Island. What town is he in?" As if I didn't know.

"East Hampton."

Great. I've just ripped out my tomatoes, rainy season is approaching, and my landscaper is summering in the Hamptons. Just great.

"I just wouldn't let it slip past Columbus Day," I warned her once I caught my breath. "After the first hard frost hits, our soil gets very slick, and your machinery is going to get stuck on the hill."

"Shouldn't be a problem," Bridget breezed. "George is pretty good with the equipment."

Sure, I wanted to tell her. So was Napoleon until he encountered Russian mud.

Poor thing (Bridget *or* Napoleon) didn't have a clue. But I had witnessed my own Waterloo after our septic system failed almost as soon as we'd moved into the house (naturally). Actually, it's not quite accurate to say our "septic system" failed. Unknown to (1) our crack home inspector, (2) the bank holding the mortgage, and (3) the novice buyers, our ninety-year-old house did not have anything resembling a septic system. In fact, I didn't even know what a septic system was. The only accommodation for waste was some ancient, brittle clay pipe that ran underground for about a hundred feet down the hill, under an old stone wall (which had partially collapsed the pipe), and into a stone well, whose exact location was a closely held secret. The liquids apparently escaped between the well stones into the surrounding soil, while the solid wastes . . . well, I don't know what became of them except that after a few months of our family's flushing the toilets, nothing was going anywhere.

We brought in Lou, a local excavator who was recommended to us by our plumber. He checked my credit, flushed some expensive transmitting device down the toilet, and listened through headphones for the plaintive beep that would reveal the location of the secret well.

It was never heard from again.

We did eventually locate and open the ancient stone tank with the help of a former owner and, after seeing it, immediately came to the conclusion that we needed a new, modern system. Within a few days, Lou had dropped in a twelve-hundred-gallon concrete holding tank and said he'd be back to complete the more time-consuming part of the system—the drainage, or leach, field—in a few weeks, after he'd completed another job. Lou explained helpfully that the way a septic system works is that all effluence goes into a concrete tank planted in your lawn. Near the very top of the tank is a pipe that leads out to a leach field, which consists of a set of underground perforated pipes. As waste enters the tank, solids drop to the bottom, where they are broken down by naturally occurring bacteria. The clean liquids on the surface flow out the pipe to the leach field, where they seep into the earth to be filtered and broken down before reentering the water table.

Grateful for the ability to flush our toilets again, we didn't fuss over the delay or even over the fact that in lieu of a drainage field for the liquid wastes, Lou had run a long hose down to the woods that constitute the lower half of our property. A little pee in the woods for a couple of weeks couldn't hurt anything. And it flowed *away* from the house.

A couple of weeks stretched into a couple of months. I started calling Lou regularly as the leaves began falling from the trees. I thought I was always polite, but Lou didn't appreciate what he felt was harassment. What had started as a cordial partnership between homeowner and contractor soon turned tense, then rancorous.

"What are you complaining about? At least you can flush your toilet," he snapped once. "Do you think I'm loafing around? I'm taking care of people who can't flush their toilets! I was there for you when you needed me, wasn't I?" He followed with a vague threat about walking off the job if I wasn't happy with him, and hung up. Uh-oh. That was the last thing I needed — to start over with a new contractor. I stopped calling.

Either in spite of, because of, or irrespective of my discontinued phone calls, one day in early November, Lou and his backhoe did materialize in the backyard and immediately started making huge gashes in the steeply sloped lawn behind the kitchen. Another day or two and the leach field would be completed.

The next morning we woke to the season's first hard frost, a sparkling carpet of silver across the grass and exposed soil. Lou arrived at 7:30 a.m. and fired up the backhoe. As I made coffee, I heard unfamiliar whining sounds coming from the machinery, not unlike the sound of a car spinning its wheels on ice. I looked out the window. The backhoe was stuck in the melting frost, the treads whirring helplessly in place. Lou came around to the house.

"I can't do anything here. I'm going to come back around noon, after the sun has dried out the ground." But the low November sun never did dry out the ground, not that day nor the next. There was once a thriving brick industry in town, and apparently a vein of brick-quality clay ran right through our property. Each morning's frost or dew brought more moisture to the clay that lay only inches below the surface of the lawn. Lou gave it a noble effort.

I watched, unbelieving, as he "walked" the backhoe up the hill by pushing the blade into the earth and lifting the treads off the ground. But clearly one could not put in a leach field by walking a backhoe around the property. Nevertheless, Lou wasn't ready to give up.

"It's supposed to get warmer next week," he explained. "Let's just leave it untouched, and I'll be back in a week to finish up."

I must have looked doubtful.

"Don't worry, we're going to get this done."

And indeed, as Lou predicted, a warm front did come in. Preceded by a thunderstorm. Torrents of water rushed through the little canyons left from the digging, leaving mud and wet, sticky clay everywhere.

Game, set, and match. Lou announced he would be back next spring to put in the leach field. We were disappointed and upset, but at least we were sure that he would keep his word, that he wouldn't walk off a job that had become a nightmare for him and for us, as some contractors might have done. In fact, we were absolutely, positively sure he'd be back.

We had his backhoe.

Right outside our kitchen window. First stuck on slick clay, then stuck in frozen clay, then covered with a blanket of snow. All fall, winter, and spring, the accusatory backhoe sat there, huge and school-bus yellow, its open jaws mocking, laughing at us, every minute we spent in the kitchen. Our Thanksgiving, Christmas, *and* Easter guests were incredulous as they stared out our kitchen window, mouths agape.

"You mean he just left it here?" was the typical response. "Is he paying you for storage?" He wasn't, of course. The hose carrying our liquid wastes down the hill also attracted some interest. I looked at our water bill and did a little math. Our typical water consumption was about six thousand gallons a month. Sounds incredible, and I can't figure out how we use all that water, but apparently that figure is typical for a family of four. Since virtually all of the water that comes into the house leaves the house via the sewage system, over the nine months between septic tank installation and leach field installation, fifty-four thousand gallons of urine, dishwater, bathwater, and anything else that went down the drain ran down our hill into the woods. Just how far down the hill that liquid got before disappearing into the ground, we never knew. We did wonder if the neighbors far on the other side of the woods ever noticed anything peculiar, but we were too chicken to ask.

As the high sun of late spring slowly dried out the clay, our uninvited guest sat motionless like a loyal pet awaiting an owner who would never return, the knuckles of its fingered scoop resting on the ground. It turned out that over the winter, Lou, who had spent his navy years in ships' boiler rooms, had been diagnosed with mesothelioma, a particularly vicious cancer of the lining of the lung. I saw him only once again. I was shocked; at first I didn't recognize him. Lou had literally become the clichéd "shell of his former self," his skin hanging too large for his emaciated body. He managed a weak, but definitely not warm, smile for me. I wished him well and shook his hand. A month later he was dead. Someone else showed up to fire up the backhoe and finish the job. But I felt, and still feel to this day, ashamed at myself for my impatience, the angry phone calls, and the ensuing bitterness. I promised myself I would never again allow a relationship with a contractor to become bitter (a promise I would break the very next year).

ALL OF WHICH IS to explain why, when Halloween approached and Bridget's husband and his Big Machinery still had not arrived, Anne, sweet Anne who absolutely hates to get involved with contractors, Anne who would rather suffer months in silence than verbalize a complaint, Anne who is totally nonconfrontational in nature, woke up and saw the frost on the pumpkin and called Bridget.

"You may know landscaping," she told a shocked Bridget, "but Bill knows his soil. You need to start this job. Now."

And a couple of weeks later, in early November, they did. I took the day off from work and anxiously awaited George and his Big Machinery. Three hours late, still breathless and blond, Bridget pulled into the driveway in her battered Toyota, followed by a flatbed truck carrying Big Machinery. A young man in his twenties, with a long, flowing blond mane and familiar crinkly green eyes got out of the truck. Bridget introduced me to Lars and explained that George was finishing up a job and would be available in a couple of days to do the "skilled" work. Meanwhile, little brother Lars's job was to pull out the brush and tear up the soil, loosening things up for the terracing operation. Bridget gave Lars a few instructions — one of which, oddly, was, "Don't drive too fast"—and was off. Lars unloaded the tractor and a disc. The disc, which I remembered seeing as a child on the TV show *Modern Farmer* very early on Saturday mornings, is a frightening device, resembling something used in the Spanish Inquisition: a two-foot-diameter metal disc that sits off kilter on a large tricycle. Hitched to the tractor, it slices deep into the soil at about a forty-five-degree angle, breaking up and loosening the earth so that it can be pushed around by other Big Machinery.

I watched from a discreet distance as Lars tried unsuccessfully to hook up the disc to the tractor, struggling with a pin-and-socket fitting. More than once, he thought he had it figured out, only to drive off and leave the disc comically behind, like a motorcycle speeding off without its sidecar. The few times it stayed attached, it bounced ineffectively over the turf. I couldn't bear to watch, so I considered offering my assistance, although I doubted I could be of much help. Even though I am the director of technology at a research institute, where I manage the computer systems, technology for me begins where machinery leaves off. Or even later. Originally an engineering major in college, I wisely switched to English literature after a frustrating freshman year spent in the basement of the engineering building, unsuccessfully struggling to get a picture on the oscilloscope. Things haven't improved much in the decades since. I'm the guy who brings his car to the dealer because I can't unfold the backseat. The most significant automotive advance of the last fifty years? My vote goes to the symmetrical car key, because until its arrival I inserted my key upside down at least half the time.

Thus I had no business helping Lars, but the poor soul looked so pathetically perplexed that I wandered over toward the tractor to offer, if nothing else, moral support. Besides, I had a question.

"Ever use one of these things, Lars?" I inquired as politely as possible.

Lars grinned somewhat guiltily and shook his blond locks from side to side.

After a few minutes of fiddling with the connection, I had it hooked up to the tractor. Lars, relieved and smiling, hopped aboard.

"Remember, Bridget said don't drive too—" He raced off, tearing around the field like a kid in a go-cart, ripping up the earth, sending clods of grass and earthworms flying. It was a horrific sight. I couldn't bear to watch. Fortunately it was growing dark by this time, so a few minutes later he climbed into his truck and drove off without doing too much damage. Oddly he never showed up again, and his name was never mentioned. Instead, a couple of days later, I arrived home from work to the sounds and smells of Big Machinery. Anne met me in the driveway.

"George is here," she said, her voice a mixture of excitement and relief.

"What's he like?"

"Handsome."

Interesting response.

Despite that flaw, and his perfect Hamptons tan underneath a trimmed beard, George was, I had to admit, instantly likable, assertive, knowledgeable, and skilled. But it was now winter on the Russian steppe, and he, like Napoleon the Emperor and Lou the Excavator before him, was no match for the brick-quality clay, his tractor slipping and sliding helplessly. If it were a horse, they would have shot it.

"I never saw anything like this," he exclaimed as he loaded his machinery onto the flatbed for the winter. At least he didn't leave it behind.

I couldn't resist getting in a parting shot. "We tried to warn you," I said. "You may know your business, but I know my land."

We Know Where You Live

Don't live in a town where there are no doctors.
—Jewish proverb

We were immigrants to this land, having fled the city of Yonkers a few years earlier in search of more breathing room. Our neighborhood in that working-class city bordering the Bronx was populated by old-school Italian and Polish families who weren't quite sure what to make of the "strangers," as we heard ourselves called. I guess we *were* strange. Anne, rather than staying home to raise kids, was putting in hundred-hour weeks as a medical resident, while I often filled both the traditional mother and father roles.

Yonkers was for us a city of contrasts. We loved our home but felt out of place in the neighborhood; we loved being able to walk to the corner market but sometimes came home numbed from the unsolicited advice of neighbors ("What is that child doing out of the house before she's been baptized!").

The most memorable advice came from a car. One night a Pontiac parked in the street woke us, warning, "Please step away from the vehicle," in a spooky Orwellian voice for hours on end, freaking out Zach, waking Anne and Katie, and very nearly inciting me to violence.

Once Anne completed her residency in internal medicine at Montefiore Hospital in the Bronx, we were free—and more than ready—to go. After a year of scouring a hundred-mile radius of New York City, we had found a wonderful small town nestled in the hills along the Hudson River, a place I nicknamed the Town That Time Forgot. Originally a farming and mill town, later a summer retreat for city dwellers, who would arrive by steamboat to be ferried to their summer homes by horse and buggy, it was a town that still took pride in its Fourth of July celebration and Memorial Day parade and had not one but two cozy libraries, a charming tavern/restaurant, and a working farm. Most important, it satisfied the two prerequisites we had set for any prospective town: a Main Street and a local newspaper, both of which we felt were essential for a sense of community, and not as easy to find as one might think. More often we found only a strip mall with a post office, a supermarket, and a pizzeria where the town center should have been. But after searching for months, we still hadn't been able to find the right house and hadn't sold our current house.

We cherished our Yonkers house, a 1910 foursquare with chestnut paneling, crown molding, and hand-cut parquet floors, and knew we wouldn't be happy in a 1960s split-level or an '80s raised ranch. Houses speak, and we had learned to listen. From our foursquare we heard the pride of the immigrant skilled laborers who had painstakingly trimmed mahogany and oak to create the decorative corners of the parquet floors, and the gaslight fixtures whispered to us of distant winter nights, inviting us to imagine the house suffused with the warm glow of gaslight. When I cleaned eighty years of cigarette smoke and grime off the chestnut paneling in the dining room, alchemically transforming it from grimy black to a warm, vibrant brown, I felt I was touching history, bringing forth new life from a species of tree now all but extinct.

In contrast, the houses we were being shown in the Town That Time Forgot were mute, without character or soul, cold modern ranches or cramped 1940s homes with neighbors within snoring distance. There were some fine older homes in town, to be sure, but they hardly ever seemed to go on the market, and the ones that did were out of our price range. It seemed hopeless.

Until we saw the Big Brown House.

We had hired a babysitter and excitedly driven up from Yonkers to see what the real estate agent had described as the perfect house for us. In the car I reminded Anne of the warning our Yonkers agent, the one trying to sell our current house, had given us. "Don't fall in love with a house before you own it. You will either be heartbroken or pay too much."

It looked as though there would be no chance of that today. The real estate agent's "perfect house" was a five-year-old prefab with all the character of a shoebox. But within sight of the shoebox, looming on the hill above, was an old, abandoned, boarded-up cedar and stone house boasting broken windows and an overgrown lawn.

"Stop here for a second," I asked the broker as we drove past on the way back to the office. "What's the deal with this place?"

She laughed at my joke and then with embarrassment realized I wasn't joking one bit and stopped the car. "It's not on the market," she said, then paused ominously. "You don't want that house." So of course we immediately did.

Anne and I went back to explore it on our own afterward, peering through gaps in the plywood that covered the windows. We could make out a fireplace, wood floors, and a wide staircase. What was the story with this abandoned house? We knocked on the door of the house next door, hoping to find out.

"You're about the fiftieth person to ask about this place," said the smiling but clearly exasperated woman who answered, understandably not happy with her role as surrogate realty agent.

"But we're actually going to buy it," I joked, trying to lighten the mood.

"Larry and I would love to see someone buy it," she said. "It's such an eyesore."

She didn't know much about the status of the house,

other than that it had not been lived in for some time. After a little detective work, I found out the house had been foreclosed on by the bank and, after years of legal proceedings, was about to go on the market "as is." We tracked down the bank's real estate agent and were the very first ones to see it.

It was a disaster. I was prepared for an abandoned house, but not for a complete dump. The previous owners had defaulted in the midst of "renovating" (a euphemism for destroying historic property). The deconstruction stage had gotten pretty far along, but the bank had lost its patience and thrown them out before they could start the *re*construction stage. We wandered around the maze of rooms on the first floor for a bit.

"Where's the kitchen?" Anne wondered after a while. We hadn't seen any rooms with, say, a stove or a sink.

Judging by the two stubby pipes sticking up out of the floor, we were standing in it. Something inspired me to tug on one of them, and it easily came free in my hand. I offered it to Anne.

"Here's the hot water. Or maybe it's the cold water."

She was not amused. She wanted this house. I could see it in her eyes; I could sense her quickening pulse. Never mind the sheets of paint peeling from the walls in every room, the floors left half-sanded when the power company literally pulled the plug on the delinquent owners. Or the rooms that had no floors at all, just bare plywood. Never mind the lack of a heating system because vandals had stolen everything they could cut or twist off the old steam boiler. Not to mention the three acres of overgrown grass, weeds, vines, and scrub trees that made it hazardous to walk in what was presumably once a yard. The listing said there was a small barn on the property; we couldn't even find it, although it would later reveal itself only one hundred feet from the house, obscured under wild grape and poison ivy, two wrecked cars rusting inside.

To Anne, these were not barriers to ownership; these were merely flaws of the house she had prematurely fallen in love with.

I could see why. It clearly had been a grand old house at one time, before falling into neglect. It was truly one of a kind—a large, rambling place (we momentarily lost each other on the first visit) with a butler's pantry and a maid's staircase, floors built of heart pine (most likely from local forests), large windows and French doors everywhere, located on a ridge with views of the Hudson River and on a clear day the Catskill Mountains. And you could walk to town, which was important to Anne.

This house desperately needed a loving owner with handyman skills and tons of free time. Anne smiled sweetly, hope and love flashing in her eyes, nominating me. "I can't do it," I said later that night, breaking her heart. I had just spent years renovating our Yonkers home, scrubbing, painting, and wallpapering, moving a load-bearing wall to make room for our newborn, Katie, building a bathroom, renovating a kitchen, and installing countless light switches and fixtures. And I had done it without help, because with Anne carrying a huge medical school debt and working in the medical profession's slave-labor pool known as residency, we were more or less broke. And to make things more difficult, it was all on-the-job learning, as I had barely touched a hammer before we bought the house. I was doing all of these fix-it jobs for the first time, studying how-to books at night, learning from mistakes during the day.

The thought of doing it again, on a scale that dwarfed the Yonkers project, was daunting. I was tired, we had a baby and a four-year-old, and we were still broke. The bank was asking a lot of money for a wreck, when you figured in the expense of adding a new roof, a heating system, plumbing, and a kitchen. I didn't think we could swing it, financially or emotionally. So for the next year we continued looking at houses, mainly ranches and colonials (whatever they are—no two seemed to have anything in common, but they were all called colonials). Anne cried on the way home one day when I became enthusiastic about a house on a secluded mountain road, because she couldn't bear the thought of not being able to walk to town. The prospect of living in that house loomed like a prison sentence to her. Soon after, she stopped seeing houses with me altogether.

"Let me know when you find something," she said flatly. "I can't do this anymore." She was really saying,

"I've found the house I want. If you want something else, you go ahead, but leave me out of it."

Anne has a tough, even unyielding, side that she rarely reveals. She saves it for big occasions, such as getting the house she wants. Or the man. I had a flashback to the day she lay down a similar gauntlet about our relationship. We had been dating exclusively for close to two years when she asked if we were going to get married. I was noncommittal.

"I'm done courting," she responded. "I'm not getting any younger." We were both thirty-one. She gave me three months to make up my mind. If I wasn't ready for marriage by then, she was moving on.

I was stunned, although I shouldn't have been. The subject of marriage had come up once before, as we were walking down Manhattan's Ninth Avenue.

"You know what tomorrow is, don't you?" Anne asked, tugging on my arm.

My mind raced. Had I forgotten her birthday? Some kind of obscure anniversary that only women remember, like our first date? I came up empty.

"Saturday?"

"Sadie Hawkins Day."

I vaguely remembered Sadie Hawkins Day from *Li'l Abner* comics, but it didn't hold any significance for me. "We're going to a square dance?"

"It's the one day a year when a woman can propose to a man," she said, studying my reaction.

And what a reaction. She got to watch the blood drain out of my face and my knees buckle slightly. She held tightly to my arm to keep me from wobbling to the pavement.

"I don't know that that would be a good idea right now," I gasped when I found my voice. "We hardly know each other." Anne erupted with something between a guffaw and a shriek. We knew each other *quite* well, and what's more, we were one of those oddball perfect matches, although I was too dense to realize it. Anne was fairly gregarious; I was a loner. Anne was a sunny optimist; I was a worrying pragmatist. I wanted to live in the country; she, in the city. Surely a match this poor couldn't help but succeed.

She teased me all the next day and even flirted with popping the question but did not propose. She was having too much fun watching me squirm to spoil the game with a marriage proposal.

But this time she was serious. Three months. I let the clock tick down to the last month before coming to my senses. I invited her to dinner at my apartment to propose. I can still remember the menu: duck with lime glaze, wild rice, baby carrots, and strawberries for dessert.

"I've been thinking about things," I said when she arrived. She knew what that meant.

"Can we have dinner first?" she asked, her voice tight, her face tense. She was sure this was to be our final date and wanted to enjoy one last meal with me. It made me wonder for a moment about her motivations for marriage: Was she looking for a good husband or a good meal?

In the end, of course, her hardball strategy won her the husband she wanted (and I hope the one she expected) and me the wife I needed. And—another example of her discipline—two remarkably timed children: Zach between medical school and residency, and Katie between residency and employment. Now, as we approached another milestone in our lives—choosing the home where we would raise our family and live our lives for the foreseeable future, maybe forever—Anne was playing tough again. But this was no mere husband we were talking about—this was a *house.*

I continued solo, seeing more raised ranches, houses built in other house's backyards, houses being rented by college kids lounging in their underwear at four in the afternoon; but every house was wrong, wrong, wrong. I found myself after each disappointing trip driving back to the old wreck on the ridge, which was still awaiting a buyer to restore it to its former glory. I'd sit in the driveway, looking at the house, the three acres, the potential for building gardens and orchards, visualizing the old barn as a future woodshop, looking for a vibe, wondering if I could muster the energy to restore this fine, neglected house. Anne had already taken a job in a city clinic outside what we were already thinking of as "our town" and was feeling the strain of commuting three hours a day. Kindergarten was fast approaching for Zach. I knew we couldn't do this much longer. And trip after trip, little by little, the house was pulling me in; it was starting to speak to me. So one day I called Anne at work and said in as casual a voice as I could muster, "What the hell, let's buy the Big Brown House." I think she cried.

I called the real estate agent. Bad news. The house had been sold just the previous week. One week. I had missed our dump-cum-dream-home by one lousy week. We moped around for a couple of days until I got a call at work.

"You still interested in the house?" our agent asked. My heart started pounding. "The buyers got cold feet and backed out. They're first-time owners, she's pregnant, and he has no handyman experience at all." What were *they* thinking? Of course we were interested. But there was a catch: Because the bank had slashed the price to unload it, five buyers already had backup bids in. If we wanted to add ours, it had to be in by five o'clock. It was now four.

"I'll get right back to you," I told her, and called Anne, who took the news with surprising sangfroid. She was not going to allow herself to be hurt again.

"We'll never beat out those other bidders," she said with a sigh.

I had a nutty idea. "Let's bid a dollar more than the asking price." This was in the midst of a real estate collapse in the Northeast, when buyers were expected to offer tens of thousands of dollars less than the asking price and usually got away with it. "No one would be crazy enough to bid the asking price for this dump," I told her. No one except us, that is, for we had defied the oracle and allowed this dump to become the House We Had to Have.

The bid strategy almost backfired because the bank figured our offer wasn't serious. They of course didn't know this wreck had become the House We Had to Have and actually tried to reject our bid, until a call from our lawyer took care of that. I'll never know for sure how much less we could have gotten the place for, but I got an idea not six months after moving in. Zach was in the local emergency room having his shoulder treated after a sledding accident. The orthopedist on call, just making conversation, asked where we lived. Anne started to describe the place.

"Not the Big Brown House!" he exclaimed. "So you're the ones who outbid me." Unsolicited, he told us his bid. Let's just say it was comforting to be in the ER at that moment.

Whether we overpaid or not, the important thing was, we owned the house, with all its possibilities for living and gardening. The twisted route by which we'd come to possess it left us with a funny feeling. It did seem just a little like fate, as if we were meant to own this house and this land.

BEFORE WE HAD EVEN moved in, it seemed that half the town knew that "a doctor and her husband" had bought the old wreck on the ridge. That is how I would come to be known—"the doctor's husband," which sounded disturbingly like an Ibsen play. Furthermore, it seemed as though everyone we met had owned, lived in, partied at, worked on, bid on, or thought of buying the Big Brown House.

Not long after moving, we went down to the firehouse to buy our Christmas tree. This is a wonderful way to buy a tree. You often run into neighbors, the firemen are very helpful and patient, you're contributing to a good cause, and they deliver free of charge without wrapping the tree in that horrible plastic netting. I'll bet they would even bring the tree inside and set it up if you asked them.

After paying for the tree, I gave the fireman our name and street address and started to give directions for delivery. He held up a hand, stopping me in midsentence.

"We know where you live," he said, looking me in the eye. "We're the fire department."

Because nearly everyone in town knew the house, I began to become more closely associated with it than I would have liked. When I met people socially, the first thing they would invariably ask was, "How's the house coming along?" and we'd have a conversation about the pine floor I was rescuing, or the carpenter bees drilling holes in the porch, or the termites eating away at the basement joists, or how I was getting up at five o'clock every morning to build kitchen cabinets before going to work.

Even going to work didn't provide an escape. My colleagues, too, wanted to talk about the house. The fact that I had taken five weeks of accumulated vacation time before moving in just to make the place livable had sparked a good deal of interest in itself. That "vacation" culminated with a good old-fashioned beam raising, when a half dozen of my male colleagues, whom I jokingly predicted were about to become "six of my ex–best friends," met at the house on a Saturday morning to raise a heavy beam that was to replace a load-bearing wall. It was their first look at the notorious house. I will never forget the first words my technical support director, a man whom I had hired and who reported directly to me, blurted out upon stepping into the house.

"Have you lost your @#&*! mind?"

Most of the people we were meeting in town probably thought so, even if they were too polite to say, and I had to give a progress report to everyone I met. This drove me crazy after a while.

"What on earth would people have to talk to me about if we didn't have this house?" I once complained to Anne. "I am not the house."

"Well," she said hesitantly. "In a sense . . ." She didn't need to finish the sentence. "And besides, you're not much of a conversationalist, you know. You don't let people into your life. The house is all they know about you. You are *defined* by the house." She let that sink in, then added, "You should really go out more."

"Thanks a lot, dear," I said, but in fact she had a point. It is true that I'm not much of a social creature. I prefer hanging around the house (which may be why finding the right house was such an obsession), doing domestic activities: cooking, woodworking, gardening, playing with the kids. Given a choice, I'd rather spend time with a lobster in the kitchen than with neighbors at a party.

Yet it still seemed a little unfair that I was fated to be defined by my property. Not by my job, not by my place in the community, but by my property. And now, after years of being defined by the house, I was about to become defined by the garden.

FINALLY, SPRING ARRIVED. In May, well after the prime planting season for potatoes, lettuce, peas, and spinach had passed, George and crew (*sans* Lars) were back. Work progressed rapidly and smoothly, and within two weeks the grassy slope had been transformed into a symmetrical, terraced kitchen garden: twenty rectangular beds, averaging four by twelve feet, plus a large area for corn and another for cucumbers, squash, and melons. All in all, nearly two thousand square feet of garden, almost as large as our living space in Yonkers. And all of it was filled with truckloads of (expensive) lush, black soil from the Hudson Valley's last brush with the Ice Age.

The garden was beautiful, the soil still fresh and black, the gravel clean. My friend Jack stopped by to survey the scene and let out a low whistle.

"Do you know what you're getting yourself into?"

I thought so, but truthfully, Anne and I really hadn't given it a lot of thought. We were a couple of kids—forty-year-old kids, but still kids—living a dream, a dream born of days wandering botanical gardens and nights poring over glossy coffee-table books. Everyone thought we were crazy when we bought an abandoned ninety-year-old country house with missing windows and no kitchen, heat, or running water, and we had proved the skeptics wrong. We were living our country life, cooking and gardening together in our restored house, and this seemed the next logical step, doing for this field of grass and weeds what we had done for the house.

"I think you're crossing the line from gardener to gentleman farmer," Jack said.

"Gentleman farmer." I liked the sound of that. *Must get suspenders*, I thought to myself.

A couple of decisions had been left for last, including the choice of shrubs for the border between our property and Larry and Claire's, and how to get water into the garden, for the nearest spigot was seventy-five feet away. Supplying water to the garden was actually the easy part; how to get it to the plants was more challenging. When we had just a single bed of tomatoes, I routinely underwatered them, not having the patience to stand outside with a hose in the evenings. How on earth was I going to water two thousand square feet? The best solution, installing drip irrigation in each bed, was naturally the most expensive as well. Anne and I debated the options. The conversation, which would become so routine in the following years as to seem almost scripted, went like this:

ME: We're already two thousand dollars overbudget. I can't see spending another thousand on irrigation. I'll run some extension hoses, and we'll water it by hand.

ANNE: That's fine. I'll help you out.

ME [*with heavy rolling of eyes*]: Just when do you plan to do that? Between making dinner, running to the hospital, and helping the kids with the homework?

ANNE: I'll work it in. I like being in the garden.

ME: Maybe we should splurge on the irrigation. It's a onetime expense. And we'll save on our water bill.

ANNE: Well, Billy [*Uh-oh, she's up to something when she calls me Billy*], what I worry about is, we built this garden to enjoy it, and if you are not going to enjoy standing out there [You? *What happened to* we?] with a hose for an hour, then we should spend the extra thousand and get the irrigation.

And then she came in with the closing argument, the bone crusher, the coup de grâce, the one that never, ever fails, because there is simply no counterargument to it.

"I'll see one extra patient a day until it's paid off."

If Anne really did this every time she used this argument, her office hours would regularly end at midnight, but I'm still a sucker for it.

"Well, if you're going to make it a gift to me . . ."

Two weeks later, exactly one week after George had laid in the sod paths, the sprinkler contractor came in and tore up the sod paths to put in underground irrigation hoses. Instead of sprinkler heads, though, we had small spigots installed at one end of each bed, from which I could attach small, quarter-inch weep hoses to run throughout the bed. It seemed like a good idea, in fact it seemed like a really smart idea, but when he left, the garden looked horrendous. There was as yet nothing growing in the beds except *faucets* sticking up everywhere— eighteen of them, on skinny black plastic pipes, looking worse than the tackiest of garden ornaments.

I vented my frustration to Anne. "I said 'a few inches.' How could he put them up so high? They look terrible!"

Anne peered out the window. "I can hardly see them."

I endured them that year, and the drip hoses were a great success, except our water bill shot up 100 percent over the summer months. This, of course, should not have been the case, because drip irrigation is the most efficient way to water. Unlike sprinklers, which lose a significant portion of their water to evaporation before it ever hits the ground, weep hoses send all the water directly into the soil. The problem is, because you can't tell when they're on—you don't see or hear anything—we were constantly forgetting to turn them off, and they often ran for hours, even overnight.

I remember one memorable trip down the New Jersey

Turnpike, on our way to Philadelphia for the weekend. The rest stops on the turnpike are named after famous (dead) Jersey residents, and to the utter dismay of my family, I can never drive past the Joyce Kilmer Rest Area without reciting the only line of verse of Joyce Kilmer's that I (or anyone else, I suspect) knows:

> I think that I shall never see
> A poem lovely as a tree.

As the Joyce Kilmer gas pumps faded in the rearview mirror, a little trigger went off in my brain, and cogs started spinning. Tree . . . plant . . . water . . . hoses. Hoses! We had left all the hoses on! A few miles down the road, we pulled into the Molly Pitcher Rest Area, where Anne used a pay phone to ask Larry (not for the last time) to turn off the hoses, while the rest of us tried to remember who the heck Molly Pitcher was. (Later research revealed she was a local hero of the American Revolution.)

There was a good snowfall the following winter, and by March we had a snow cover of over eighteen inches. I started peeking out of the kitchen window daily, monitoring the progress of the melt, eager to start the leaf lettuces and especially the potatoes. As the snow gradually receded, I started to see brass faucets peeping up one by one through the snow, like little brass sparrows. Very cute. This was soon followed by skinny black pipes, growing longer each day, vividly stark against the white snow. Not so cute. Nothing else was visible in the garden, just eighteen black pipes topped by faucets—no longer sparrows—poking erectly, obscenely, hideously through the snow.

"It won't look so bad once the snow melts," Anne reassured me.

But it did. Against the starkness of an empty March garden, it looked like I was growing a crop of plastic pipes. The irony of it! Me, snobbish Mr. All Natural Materials, who prefers plaster to Sheetrock, cotton to polyester, cedar to pressure-treated wood—I had a garden that resembled an abandoned oil field.

I couldn't take it. I went out with the pipe cutter, some couplings, and a can of PVC cement. I cut the pipes down one by one so that the spigots were just a few inconspicuous inches off the ground. Then I started to attach the hoses to the spigots. Except I couldn't. I had forgotten that the hoses couldn't make a ninety-degree angle under the spigots; they had to make a gradual curve. In my zeal to cut down the pipes, I hadn't left enough room. In the end I had to scoop out handfuls of soil beneath each spigot, and I still curse under my breath every time I have to struggle to attach a hose. As it turns out, if I had just been patient, the original height wouldn't have been too bad. We've since planted a row of thyme down the edges of the beds where the spigots are, and the thyme obscures the faucets to the extent that I sometimes lose one and have to dig around in the tangly thyme to locate it.

Patience in the garden is a good thing. (I must try to remember that.)

ONE FINAL PIECE of garden construction remained before I was ready to fence it all in: the border between our garden and the neighbors' property. The garden, lovely as it was, was lacking one important feature. Privacy. Because the garden was sunken, Larry's property — the asphalt parking area/basketball court, the kitchen deck, and the garden shed — loomed directly over it, giving us the feeling of always being watched. We were probably more entertaining than television. I could just imagine the conversations they had.

"Hey, Claire, come watch this. Bill is *replanting* all the tomatoes that Anne put in this morning."

"How can she stand it? I give this marriage another six months."

(For your information, Larry and Claire, Anne planted the tomatoes too shallow. I had no choice.)

Anyway, ours was decidedly *not* the Secret Garden. So Bridget had wisely designed a hedge, a hedge of Emerald arborvitae. On the one hand, this wasn't such a bad idea, as you can buy them already seven feet tall — instant privacy — and they grow so slowly that maintenance is almost nonexistent. And being evergreen, they provide a year-round screen.

On the other hand, there was the price tag: $3,500. And deer love them. As proof, they had gnawed to stubs the three that Larry had already planted. Even though the garden would be fenced, almost no fence is deerproof. Why invite trouble? I couldn't see spending $3,500 to have it go to deer food. I asked Bridget about other options.

"What about privet?" I asked. "You see great privet hedges in all the English gardens, and in the Hamptons."

"You can only buy them two feet tall," Bridget replied, "and they are very slow growing."

In other words, I would be dead before they made a respectable hedge.

"You mean to tell me that all of the privet on Further Lane"—I tossed out one of the haute addresses in East Hampton—"are twenty years old? Around those brand-new houses?"

Bridget just shrugged into the phone. She was not interested in privet.

I was in a quandary. We needed something low maintenance and slow growing and not too expensive. Then one morning a newspaper ad for a nursery out in the western end of the county caught my eye. It had seven-foot arborvitae at a price of less than half what Bridget had quoted us. Even though we rarely venture out into that part of the county, I got out the map and decided to go take a look. It was a miserable day, with intermittent pouring rain and poor visibility, and I didn't know where this discount nursery was—just somewhere along the two-lane highway. And suddenly, through the drizzle and fog, there it was, immediately ahead, on the left side of the highway. To keep from driving by, I instinctively hit the turn signal and braked hard to wait for traffic from the opposite direction to clear. The car behind me braked hard. And the car behind that. And the car behind that.

I made the left turn into the parking lot and got out of the car. And that's when I noticed the commotion. Traffic on the highway had come to a halt, people were out of their cars, and a woman was pointing at me. "It's all his fault," I heard her say. With a sickening feeling growing in my stomach, I took in the scene: The car directly behind me had been rear-ended, as had the next two cars behind that. I had caused a three-car accident by stopping suddenly on a rain-slicked road. No one was hurt, thank goodness. All of the drivers were out of their cars, standing in the pouring rain, fuming. I tried to look inconspicuous, but at six feet four inches, that is next to impossible. I weighed my options as sweat suddenly burst from every pore, puddling under my vinyl slicker. I could cross the street, fess up, and face the angry mob (not to mention their lawyers); I could continue innocently browsing among the arborvitae as if nothing had happened ("Who, me?"); or I could get the hell out of there.

Talk about your ethical dilemmas. I wasn't enthusiastic about facing the mob. It would have been the honest thing, the courageous thing, even the *right* thing to do, but at the time it sure didn't seem like the smartest. Besides, I told myself, the fact that the car directly behind me was able to stop without hitting me proved that I had not done anything reckless. The cars behind *him* were following too closely and too fast on slick roads. I may have *precipitated* the accident, but I wasn't *responsible* for it, I told myself, though such rationalization did little to diminish the guilt.

On the other hand, hopping back in the car and running away seemed like a blatant admission of culpability, so rather by default I ended up exercising the middle option: wandering around the garden center as if nothing had happened, while I pondered my next move. My head was pounding, my stomach was nauseated, a cold sweat was drenching me. I thought, *So this is what it feels like.* I was thinking about Raskolnikov after he'd bludgeoned the old woman to death in *Crime and Punishment.* I tried to keep out of view of the highway as I looked at a couple of shrubs, but I was just going through the motions. I didn't even know what I was looking at. I heard one of the nursery workers say, "Third accident this year." That made me feel better; I could at least attribute some of the blame to poor highway design. "Another damn fool stopping too suddenly!" he added, looking directly at me. I nodded weakly in agreement.

Time to leave. Stoop-shouldered, I made my way to my car, ducking behind shrubs as best I could, calmly pulled out of the lot, and drove very carefully home. Half a mile down the road I passed several police cars, sirens blaring, heading toward the accident—*my* accident. I kept checking my rearview mirror during the forty-five-minute drive, expecting to be tracked down and pulled over at any moment, but I made it home without incident, where I stayed in the shower until the hot water ran out. What a stupid, ill-conceived venture. I never did find out what their arborvitae were like, but I swore never to venture into foreign territory again just to find a bargain. I would stay close to town from now on.

The next morning I ran out to get the newspaper at six o'clock and flipped through it furiously, looking for a story about a driver leaving the scene of an accident. Nothing. I exhaled deeply. It was, after all, just a minor fender bender (okay, three) on a day that probably saw dozens of them, not the crime of the century that my guilt and fear had built it up to be. Nevertheless, I didn't rest easy for weeks afterward. And I still had to decide on a hedge.

"How many extra patients do you have to see to pay for thirty-five hundred dollars' worth of arborvitae?" I asked Anne.

"As many sessions of psychotherapy as you're going to need when the deer start eating them," was her reply. "Don't you think you're spending a little too much time on this?" she added, hinting at my growing obsession. Weeks had gone by, and I still hadn't come to a decision, which Anne had left to me while she did silly things like heal the sick.

She was right. I settled on forsythia, tightly spaced and

trimmed as a neat hedge. The whole thing cost less than seven hundred dollars, and although I have to go at them with hedge trimmers two or three times a year, they grew to seven or eight feet in no time at all and provide great privacy and a brilliant wall of yellow in the spring. And the deer don't seem interested in them.

With the forsythia installed, the kitchen garden was basically complete. It wasn't perfect, it wasn't exactly what we'd dreamed of, but as Anne and I stood overlooking it, champagne in hand, it appeared magnificent, enticing, beckoning. It seemed to say, "Come, bring me your seeds and water, and I will reward you." And it would. And also humble me, and teach me, and become a place of solace, a battleground, a source of pride, a source of frustration, a time sink, a respite.

Anne offered a modest and unusual toast: "That wasn't so bad, was it?"

I looked at her quizzically, then offered my own: "Wonder what ever happened to Lars."

One Man's Weed Is
Jean-Georges's Salad

*There's only one sure way to tell the weeds from
the vegetables. If you see anything growing,
pull it up. If it grows again, it was a weed.*
— Corey Ford, "Advice to the Home Gardener,"
Look, September 2, 1954

Alone in my new garden, kneeling over a bed filled
with rich, dark brown topsoil dug from the glacial deposits of the Hudson Valley, I scooped up a handful
of soil and took in its earthy, almost aphrodisiac smell.
Ahh. I love the smell of earth. No perfume ever invented
by man has matched the smell of rich, loamy soil. Maybe
it was worth it after all—the arguments, the agonizing de-
lays, the cost overruns. Yes, it was worth it. I scanned the
empty beds and saw bloodred tomatoes, tall stalks of corn
waving in the sun, snow-white heads of cauliflower. It was
good. I was happy.

A disembodied voice from above startled me out of my
reverie.

"Gonna be a lot of weeding."

What the—did the garden come with its own Greek chorus? I looked up and saw Larry's head peering down into the garden over the newly planted forsythia.

"Excuse me?" I wasn't sure I had heard him right. Maybe he had really said, "Gorgeous garden. It's going to be beautiful to gaze upon it from our kitchen window."

"Gonna be a lot of weeding," he repeated. I let the handful of sixty-dollar-a-yard topsoil drop back into the bed.

"Cultivating," I said under my breath. "Gonna be a lot of *cultivating.*"

What's the difference?

Well, none, really. Except image. As when decades ago my sweaty teenage sister (or was it Blanche DuBois?) declared, "Ah don't sweat; ah perspire." Well, ah don't weed; ah cultivate. (As it turns out, ah will cultivate *a lot.*) Whereas *weeding* evokes images of backbreaking labor, kneeling under a broad-brimmed hat while hand-yanking weeds into a basket to be dumped in a remote corner of the yard, *cultivating* suggests nurturing, caring for tender shoots, feeding, and raising. All of which you accomplish, of course, by kneeling and hand-yanking weeds into a basket to be dumped in a remote corner of the yard.

I dismissed Larry with a laugh and a wave, but the fact was, I didn't have a clue as to how I was going to keep twenty-two beds weeded when in the past I hadn't even kept our small tomato bed clean. While we were planning the garden, I assured myself it wasn't really twenty-two beds. Zach and Katie would surely each want to have a bed or two of their own—the "children's garden"—so that left me with maybe only eighteen. And part of our crop-rotation strategy (rotation is important to maintaining healthy soil) was to leave up to four beds fallow each year, so it was really only fourteen beds, not twenty-two. And Anne would be helping. So maybe the number was more like ten. Whew! That sounded a lot more manageable. Besides, I figured I had time before I had to deal with weeds. The garden was filled with virgin topsoil. Surely I would have a year's grace period before weed spores came in on the northwesterly winds that sweep up our ridge?

Except that not only was this topsoil not virgin, it was a veritable tramp. By the first warm weather, the beds were covered with tiny ground-cover plants that I had never seen before. They didn't come from *my* neighborhood. They could only have hitchhiked in with the soil. Then other weeds started arriving—plantain, bindweed, bitter cress. Weeds that looked like mesclun sprouted up alongside my mesclun. Weeds that looked like baby-carrot tops sprouted up in my carrot bed. (How *do* they do that?) At first I really didn't mind; I enjoyed being in the beds, on my hands and knees, taking in the late-spring sunshine and sweet-smelling soil. I was living my dream. But it didn't take long for the dream to start feeling like a nightmare. I was spending hours a week weeding—I mean, cultivating—by hand.

All *twenty-two* beds, not ten. For over the winter, finding that we were, even with this huge space to work with, once again agonizing over what to plant and what to leave out, we had ended up filling every bed. I really wanted to try arugula, and Anne had always yearned for endive, and neither of us wanted to wait till next year. So, like a couple of kids in a candy store, we bought both. And so on.

The plans for the children's garden didn't fare much better. For Easter, instead of chocolate bunnies, Zach and Katie got their very own set of kid-size garden tools, a "gardening for kids" book, and kid-size garden gloves. And the real treat: the news that they could each have their own garden and plant anything they wanted in it!

They couldn't have been less enthusiastic if we had given them each a pick and shovel and told them they'd be working in the mines from now on instead of going to school.

"Do we have to?" moaned Zach, who viewed every minute outdoors as a minute away from his computer.

Katie at least feigned interest, but it was clear she would've preferred a bunny—real or chocolate.

But we weren't ready to throw in the towel. Having forgotten every lesson from our own childhoods, we figured that surely once they had tried gardening, they, too, would be hooked.

In my case, even though my father was passionate about his tomatoes and apples, I couldn't have been less interested in gardening when I was Zach's age. Perhaps observing my father's fervor planted the seeds of my own passion, but they didn't sprout until, in my early twenties, in a post-Watergate, postcollegiate, living-in-my-parents'-basement funk, I clipped an intriguing job ad and, next thing I knew, found myself teaching high school math in the U.S. Virgin Islands. I was amazed to find that on St. Thomas, where agriculture could be practiced twelve months of the year, there was virtually no fresh produce to be found. Everything was shipped in from the States or Puerto Rico and, as often as not, arrived spoiled.

My studio apartment in a private home was located on a lush hillside, and within a couple of weeks of moving in, I obtained permission from my landlady to clear about thirty square feet of wild tropical vegetation for a vegetable garden. Certainly the desire for fresh vegetables was a motivating factor, but, a little homesick and unsure of the wisdom of my latest, somewhat impulsive career move, I also received a great deal of comfort from that garden. Perhaps starting a garden was also a way of subconsciously staking my claim, announcing my arrival in this new land and declaring a measure of permanence. The garden served yet another purpose: I used it almost immediately as an excuse for not being able to attend a faculty get-together at the beach. I was prevailed upon to show up at the party, but I had set the precedent of declaring my preference for the solitary pleasures of gardening over social events.

Anyway, for some reason Anne and I just assumed that

the kids would be interested in gardening and even excited at the prospect of a bed of their own.

"Just give it a try," Anne said enthusiastically. "You may like it. Now let's talk about what you're going to plant this year."

"What do you mean, *this* year?" Zach asked warily.

Anne explained that vegetable gardens have to be planted every spring, as the plants die off during the winter. This was frightful news to them both.

"Isn't there anything we can plant just once?" they pleaded.

"Well, there's rhubarb," I offered. "Or asparagus."

The alarm grew on their faces.

"Strawberries," Anne added, averting a crisis.

So our children's garden consisted of two beds of strawberries. The kids did help plant them, if reluctantly, and even enjoyed picking—and eating—them. The following season, Anne and I were treated to the wonderful sight of Katie and her friends collecting and eating strawberries, filling up baskets with the plump berries, a Norman Rockwell scene that was rerun repeatedly over a span of two weeks, since the berries ripened almost as fast as they could pick them. We had a huge crop that year, more than enough to split with Katie's friends and share with neighbors, with plenty left over for breakfast cereal and wonderful strawberry shortcakes.

The strawberries took care of two of the beds on the planting and harvesting side, but all the gardening in between—namely weeding—we couldn't get the kids to do without dragging them into the garden, practically kicking and screaming. It didn't seem worth it. Thus, when all was said and done, Anne and I—mostly I—were weeding twenty-two beds by hand and falling behind quickly. I was ready to try something else to control weeds, something that would prevent them from sprouting in the first place: the barrier method.

There are a couple of ways to do this, but the approach that I tried (and that many farmers use) involves laying a physical weed block on the soil. This is the condom approach to prevention, and it does have its strong points. Weeds will definitely not grow through plastic. Slugs don't like it, either. And the weed block (usually black) warms the soil and can produce earlier crops. In the large vine bed, where we were planting melons, cucumber, and squash, I cut a sheet of heavy black plastic to fit the bed and weighed the edges down with a few stones. Then I sliced openings where I was planting the seedlings or seeds. I did the same in one of the lettuce beds, but because I was sowing almost continuous rows of minuscule lettuce seeds, punching holes was impractical. Instead I cut the plastic into strips, leaving a couple of inches for the seeds between each strip.

Anne preferred a different barrier method. One afternoon I came into the garden to find her kneeling over the rhubarb bed with a tall stack of the *New York Times.*

"All the news that's fit to plant?" I wisecracked.

"Very funny."

"What on earth are you doing?"

"Using newspaper and grass clippings to keep the weeds out."

More than likely planting the seeds of disaster. "Please don't do this," I begged.

"Why? I used to do this at my parents' house. It's a common method."

"Because it's going to end up a big mess, and we'll have a fight."

"Only if you start one."

Undeterred, she laid down thick layers of newspaper topped with several inches of dried grass clippings.

The first year was okay (if a little ugly), but by the following spring the newspaper had decomposed and become interspersed with the brown grass clippings and fresh weeds, giving the bed the appearance of a garbage dump. We had a brief fight of the "I told you so" variety.

Truthfully, I wasn't any happier with my plastic. Before long I came to two conclusions about the barrier method: (1) it works, and (2) I'd rather have weeds. The plastic looked horrendous in the garden—shiny black, with puddles of standing water for days after every rain. And it was horrible to walk on. Some gardeners hide the plastic with a cover of grass clippings, but I think that looks almost as bad, and smells worse. Others prefer to use "landscape fabric," which is less shiny and allows water to permeate, but eventually weeds also permeate, coming up right through the fabric, and then you never get them out.

In the rhubarb bed, I cleaned up the paper and grass and laid in a good, thick layer of dark bark mulch. This did suppress weeds, but to the neighborhood cats it said "kitty litter." You can guess the rest. So much for dark bark.

My biggest objection to the barrier method wasn't the appearance or even the kitty magnet. I missed the soil. I didn't spend a thousand bucks on beautiful, sweet-smelling glacial soil to cover it in plastic, fabric, news-paper, or mulch. These materials isolate you from the earth, from the feel and smell of the soil, from the garden-ing experience. The metaphor was not misplaced: it was *exactly* like having sex wearing a condom.

I did love unprotected gardening. I never wore gloves. I exalted in my rich, black topsoil. I loved the feel of it. I loved the fact that on a chilly but sunny spring day the soil was warmer than the air, that kneeling in it was comfort-ing and warming. I delighted in finding earthworms, the gardener's best friend, wiggling among the potatoes. So over the winter, I pondered the whole issue again. As I considered the various approaches, I came up with four basic strategies for dealing with weeds: Prevent, Elimi-nate, Control, or Ignore.

Having already discarded (for the time being, at least) prevention, I was left with the three remaining options.

To eliminate weeds, you must get the root—the whole root—out of the ground. This is the route that Anne and most suburban gardeners take. She lets the weeds grow for weeks until she can't stand looking at them anymore (that is, when they're obscuring her flowers), then disappears into the garden in her straw hat and gloves, wielding a weapon called, not surprisingly, a weeder or weeding fork. (Note that it is *not* generally called a cultivator.) This tool consists of a hard wooden or plastic handle with a steel rod that terminates in a broad, forked prong. With this device, you stab into the soil and get the blade under the root of the weed, then try to push the root up with a wiggle motion as you yank out the weed with the other hand. Drop the intact weed into a basket, and repeat. And repeat. And repeat. And repeat. For each weed. Anne does this literally until blisters on her hand make it too painful to continue. A month or so later, she has to do it all over again. Yet somehow she is sold on this technique, flirtations with newspaper mulch aside.

But she was mainly tending only the few flower and herb beds, leaving me with what is botanically called "the rest"—that is, the tomatoes, cucumbers, squash, lettuce, spinach, carrots, leeks, potatoes, endive, snap peas, green beans, arugula, squash, and corn. I'm not quite sure how this informal division of labor came about. We never discussed it, and I certainly hadn't planned on it, but a pattern had quickly, quietly emerged: I was the vegetable gardener, and Anne was the flower and herb gardener. This was fine in principle, except that the garden was predominantly a *vegetable* garden, so the division of labor was unexpectedly weighted heavily in my favor.

Labor aside, for the most part this specialization of roles has worked out well over the years, and Anne and I make a good pair in the garden, her yin complementing my yang. Anne can keep our kitchen supplied with herbs throughout the year, growing, drying, and bottling thyme, lavender, oregano, and savory. I can build a compost heap that literally steams, turning oak leaves and horse manure into sweet, crumbly compost in six months. Anne is skilled with the flowers and knowledgeable about their habits. I can't remember any of their names (common *or* Latin), especially the *p* flowers: petunia, pansy, peony, poppy, potentilla, even im*p*atiens. It is not unusual for me to find myself caught in an embarrassing sentence like, "Isn't that a nice — uh, you know, *p* flower." Which doesn't give me much credibility as a gardener.

This de facto specialization, however it evolved, did leave me with a lot of weeding, and I realized early on that if I was going to survive, I had to become more efficient at it. Anne could get away with a weeding fork in the flower beds she was tending, but if I were to weed the vegetable beds this way, weeding the garden would be like painting the George Washington Bridge. To New Yorkers, it seems that work crews are *always* painting the George

Washington Bridge. They never finish, because by the time they work their way to the east end, the west end needs repainting. I had to find a better way.

Having had no success with prevention or elimination, my two remaining options were to control the weeds or to ignore them. While ignoring weeds sounds uncomfortably close to another strategy, one called *giving up,* it shouldn't be dismissed out of hand. Why not just leave them? I know the argument, and it sounds pretty convincing—that weeds rob your vegetables of precious nutrients from the soil. But how do we know that there aren't enough nutrients for all? A little kelp extract or the occasional buried fish ought to take care of that. How do we know that weeds in close proximity to broccoli don't have some *beneficial* effect, like keeping aphids away or something? Certainly in the extreme case, if you let weeds get out of hand, they will crowd out your plants and block off sunlight as well, but aside from appearance, is there really any harm in letting a few weeds sprout up between your tomatoes? Not according to one small farmer in California I read about who had stopped weeding his garden, which supplies organic greens to the trendiest West Coast restaurants.

It was tempting. Very tempting. The next year, I did a trial, letting the corn bed (about three hundred square feet) go weedy. What a disaster! I never got to find out if the corn minded, because *I* minded so much. By midsummer, weeds of every variety had spread so voraciously and rapidly that the land—and my expensive glacial top-

soil—seemed to be threatening to return to nature.
Things must be different in California (duh!). I bit the
bullet and spent four hours on my hands and knees with
Anne's weeding fork, painstakingly pulling out every
weed. When I finished, I had a blister the size of a quarter on my palm, but the bed looked beautiful again, rows
of corn separated by strips of clean, weed-free soil.

Having now discarded preventing, eliminating, and ignoring them, the only remaining option was to control
them. Which is how I eventually, inevitably, came to fall
in love with the hoe. I say "inevitably" because the hoe
turns out to be my kind of tool, a tool steeped in history,
reverently represented in art and literature. A real gentleman farmer's kind of tool, the farmer's equivalent of the
woodworker's chisel.

The hoe was probably the first farming tool invented.
Wooden hoes are believed to have been used in the Paleo-
lithic era, around 9000 BC. Even into the twentieth century, the hoe has retained a certain nobility, a symbolism
of hard, virtuous, and backbreaking work.

Perhaps the most famous painting depicting a hoe is
L'Homme à la houe, or *Man with a Hoe*, completed by
Jean-François Millet in 1862. It is a bleak painting, depicting a downtrodden French peasant with a strong body
but a prematurely old, exhausted face, leaning heavily on
his hoe in his hopelessly rocky, weedy field. Millet himself wrote of hoeing, "Is this the gay, jovial work some
people would have us believe in? But nevertheless, to me

it is true humanity and great poetry." The painting, which was widely interpreted as a socialist protest about the plight of the peasant, created a storm of controversy in Europe. It gained an audience in America in 1899 when Edwin Markham, after seeing the painting, published his poem "The Man with a Hoe" in William Randolph Hearst's *San Francisco Examiner*. Here is the opening stanza:

> Bowed by the weight of centuries he leans
> Upon his hoe and gazes on the ground,
> The emptiness of ages in his face,
> And on his back, the burden of the world.
> Who made him dead to rapture and despair,
> A thing that grieves not and that never hopes,
> Stolid and stunned, a brother to the ox?
> Who loosened and let down this brutal jaw?
> Whose was the hand that slanted back this brow?
> Whose breath blew out the light within this brain?

Wow. No starry-eyed romantic view of farming *here*. The poem was reprinted widely and struck a nerve with an American public recovering from the stock market crash of 1893 and facing the closing of the American frontier. Pundits from William Jennings Bryan to Ambrose Bierce weighed in on the ensuing fierce debate on labor and society, while the wits of the day published poetic parodies such as "The Man with the Dough" and "The Man with the Lawnmower."

With a history like this, the hoe was destined to wind

up in my hands, the hands of an English major, better designed for turning pages in a book than for turning over
the soil. When I picked up a hoe, I felt connected not only
to the land but also to some of my favorite painters, such
as Millet, Seurat, and Brueghel. The hoe is designed to either cut through or lift up the roots of weeds and bring
them to the surface (along with a fresh supply of previ-
ously dormant weed spores). But unlike a hand weeder, a
hoe at least allows you to stand up.

If you stand less than five feet tall, that is. Here is one
of my pet peeves, and I hope somewhere a tool manufac-
turer is reading this and taking note. All hoes, as well as
most other garden tools, are made with five-foot handles.
Anyone of average height (and I am well above average,
thank you) cannot stand up straight and comfortably use
a hoe or a rake with a five-foot handle. This isn't 1780,
when people slept in those impossibly short beds you see
in historic homes. America has grown up (physically, at
least). We're all taller, but the tools we use are still made
for Dolley Madison.

This is why many people consider hoeing backbreaking work. The hoes are simply too short. Of course, it *is*
backbreaking work anyway, because you have to use a lot
of strength to pull a flat blade with twenty to thirty square
inches of surface area through the soil, particularly heavy,
clayey soil. I often felt (and looked) like Millet's man after a few minutes with a hoe. Until I discovered the stirrup hoe.

The stirrup hoe, also called the oscillating, Appalachia, or shuffle hoe (buyer beware: several different styles of hoe are called shuffle hoes) has a U-shaped steel blade that swings through a small arc on the end of its too-short wooden handle. In fact, it looks just like a stirrup on a stick. As you draw it toward you, the blade runs under the soil and slices the weed (or whatever else is in its path) several inches below the surface. With a standard hoe, at the end of your draw, you must lift the hoe out of the soil, push it away from you, and make another stab into the soil. With the stirrup hoe, you can leave it in the ground and continue working it from and toward you, because it is effective with either a draw or a push stroke. Thus the name *shuffle hoe.*

There's only one problem: except for shallow weeds, which the stirrup may bring up, roots and all, in one piece, all this shuffling and slicing hasn't removed or even killed a single weed. If anything, this hard pruning may make the weed come back even stronger, and perhaps with multiple shoots replacing the single one severed. But remember, this is the "weed *control*" strategy of cultivation. It's what farmers have been doing for thousands of years. True, the weed will come back, but if you cultivate on a regular basis (say, weekly), the weeds will never get established and threaten your vegetables or flowers. Because it doesn't have a large, flat blade, it requires much, much less force to use than a standard hoe, and it doesn't turn over the soil, bringing fresh weed spores to the surface. On a warm summer morning, it can be a downright pleasant and even soothing activity, as you get into a nice, easy back-and-forth rhythm. Now, *this* is cultivating. If only the handle were a foot longer, I could use it comfortably.

I keep my stirrup hoe clean and dry. Its effectiveness is dependent on its sharp blade. One does have to be careful with a good stirrup hoe. It doesn't know a tomato plant from a knotweed, and more times than I'd like to admit, my gentle to-and-fro rhythm has been punctuated by a piercing scream when I realize I've gotten careless and whacked off a corn stalk. Or a Brandywine tomato. Or a drip irrigation hose. I've killed them all.

WEED REVISIONISM (MY OWN TERM) was all the rage a few years back. It was hard to pick up a garden magazine without encountering a weed apologist. Under weed-revisionist theory, weeds are not inherently "bad." They are only "bad" because they happen to be growing where you don't want them. In other words, the revisionist's definition of a weed is "a plant considered undesirable in its present location." In fact, although this belief was popular in the 1990s, it was Ralph Waldo Emerson who said a hundred years earlier, "What is a weed? A plant whose virtues have not yet been discovered." Still, all of this weed revisionism had always seemed to me like a bunch of nonsense. My definition of a weed is somewhat narrower. A weed is usually (but not necessarily) unattractive, always invasive, difficult to eradicate, *and* undesirable in its present location.

But something happened recently to make me reconsider revisionism: The corn bed, because it is in the lower, nonterraced area of the garden, is not a raised bed. Thus it never received the glacial topsoil that the rest of the beds did when the garden was constructed, and the native soil there is the heavy clay typical of our property. After a few years of struggling with it, I decided to make it a raised bed and asked our landscaper Carmine to add eight inches of a fifty-fifty mix of topsoil and compost. Naturally, being a landscaper (fancy title for "the guy who cuts the grass"), he ignored me and instead dumped — well, you can't really call it topsoil — pure *dirt.* No compost. And the dirt he put in wasn't appreciably better than what was already there. Now I just had more of it.

I was steamed at Carmine — again. The previous year I had asked him to plant two pine trees to give us more privacy on the porch. We had plenty of trees on the property but no pine, and I wanted to be able to clip my own boughs for decorating the house at Christmas. Normally I would have gone to the nursery and selected the trees myself, but feeling overwhelmed, I took what seemed to be the reasonable shortcut of letting my landscaper select and plant the trees. In other words, the way I imagine many homeowners do it.

I came home one day to find a pair of seven-foot fir trees

planted in the ground. Not pine, *fir.* I know that a lot of lay-people make this mistake and call every evergreen tree they see a pine, but I did expect a little better of my landscaper. Not wanting to cause financial hardship for him, I let it slide. But to this day, every Christmas, I look out the window, lamenting, "I really wanted a pine tree."

Sometimes it seems as though I can't win. If I insist on doing everything myself or overseeing every last detail, I'm obsessive, controlling, and stressed out. If I try to let go a little and delegate, the job is botched, which ends up causing even *more* stress. If there's a middle ground to this dilemma, I haven't found it. But with hundreds of dollars of worthless dirt in my corn bed and a pair of fir trees needling me from the porch, I figured that firing Carmine was a step in the right direction.

"We can't," Anne said after I'd presented my case. "He and his wife are patients."

"So?"

"I can't fire a patient. How awkward would that be the next time Carmine or his wife came to my office?"

"Half the people in town are your patients. That's quite a restriction you're putting on us."

"We are not firing him. Besides, have you forgotten that no one else will cut our grass?"

Well, that wasn't quite true. But it *was* true that we had already run through just about all the landscapers who would. Our sloping, irregularly shaped lawn is a little challenging. When I was phoning around for a new landscaper a few years earlier, Carmine was the only one who hadn't said, "You mean the Big Brown House?" and hung up.

Most of the landscapers in town were born and raised here and never left. Maybe played a little football on the high school team, got their diplomas, didn't know of any other place they'd rather live (understandably), so they stayed right here in the Town That Time Forgot and managed to scrape together a living out of cutting other people's lawns. A few of them became rather successful, over time expanding their solo ventures into full-fledged enterprises with several trucks and a staff; others remained one-man operations, a guy with a lawn mower. But all of the ones we met had one thing in common: "In high school I used to come here and drink in that field," they would reminisce, pointing to what was now Larry's yard, "look at the river, and get drunk."

Our first landscaper, who sported uncombed hair and taped-together eyeglasses that sat askew on his face, escalated that tradition into adulthood, stopping traffic on a major Hudson River bridge for hours one day when he climbed the superstructure with a six-pack and refused to come down. This behavior disturbed but did not surprise Anne, who always felt uncomfortable in his presence and was suspicious of his uncanny knack for showing up on her day off, which varied.

"I don't like the way he looks at me," she had complained.

"What way is that?"

"Like a dog eyeing a raw piece of liver."

His successor insisted, despite our repeated pleading, on blowing the grass clippings *toward* the house after each cut, his leaf blower shooting a hundred-mile-an-hour jet of grass, dirt, pollen, and dust through the numerous cracks and gaps in our ninety-year-old house. We found ourselves having to dust and vacuum after each cutting. Once, he used a rope of mine to tow his mower out of the wet clay he had wandered into after a heavy rain. This would have been fine, except the rope was part of a rustic tree swing I had meticulously built for the kids, risking life and limb (mine, that is) to tie it to a branch some thirty feet high. When I saw the sixty feet of flaccid rope, loosely coiled on the ground, I almost cried.

With our checkered history of landscapers, I let Anne convince me that we couldn't fire a patient (as if I had a choice), and Carmine stayed. Until a few years later, when he fired *us*, without even telling us; the grass just kept growing taller and taller, he wouldn't return our calls, and finally we concluded he wasn't coming back. We had to scramble to find a new landscaper, in the middle of summer no less. Anne saw Carmine in her office shortly after.

"So just how awkward was it?" I asked.

"Not very. He acted like nothing had happened."

I tried to amend the corn bed's twenty-four-dollar-a-yard dirt with homemade compost when I could, but after a few years of heavy corn crops, the soil was looking and acting exhausted. It was time to revitalize it. I had been reading about what are called green manures—that is, crops that you grow to turn into and enrich the soil—and decided to give it a try. A couple of seed houses sell green-manure mixes, usually containing things such as legumes and oats and other annual species that will not come back the next year after you've turned them in.

My plan was to get in an early planting of the green-manure mix, turn it into the soil in June, then follow immediately with a second planting, this one consisting of scattered dwarf marigolds to give us some color through the summer. I chose dwarf marigolds precisely because they are dwarf; in the fall I planned to mow and mulch them, then turn them into the soil as well. The family griped about a year without corn.

"You want us to eat the farmstand corn?" Zach cried, indignant.

This was getting interesting.

"Do you guys realize that city folks drive an hour and a half for that farmstand corn?" I said.

"It's not as good as yours," Katie grumbled, "and corn has to be cooked within a half hour of picking."

I was taken off guard by their resistance. But I gave them the Dust Bowl ("See what happens if you don't replenish the soil?") speech, and that quelled the uprising.

The whole project—the green-manure mix and the marigold seeds—was going to cost the price of a couple of yards of composted cow manure, which probably would have been far more beneficial to the soil, but I wanted to try green-manuring, and I was not to be deterred by logic or cost.

In April I cleared the bed of weeds, planted the oat, clover, and sweet-pea seeds, gave them a good soaking with the hose—and waited for something to come up. I didn't know what the germination period was for these things, but peas are usually pretty quick. A couple of weeks went by and the bed was still bare. Finally I saw a few peas. Then some other seedlings started coming up. Lots of them. This is good, right? I wasn't so sure. These seedlings looked familiar, like a weed I'd seen around. But how could I tell? Was it weed or expensive seed? I looked for the plant in a textbook but couldn't find it. I decided to take a wait-and-see attitude. Eventually I started seeing this plant in other beds, and I realized it was indeed a weed. Nothing germinated from my expensive green-manure mix but a handful of peas, possibly because of drought conditions, compounded by my inattention to watering. I'd had to resort to hand watering—never my forte—as drip hoses are effective only for rows of plants, not the wide scattering of seeds that I had dispersed. Of course, the *weed* had no trouble at all germinating and flourishing in a drought, but (revisionists take note) that's what makes it a weed.

In June, with some difficulty, I turned this pea-weed crop into the soil with a pitchfork, questioning again my reluctance to purchase a small tiller. (I stubbornly adhere to the belief that there is no place for a noisy, smelly gasoline engine in a garden.) As I was planting the marigold seeds, I read the back of the seed packet for the first time: "Days to flower: 90." It was June 15. My marigolds, which were supposed to give us color all summer, weren't even going to bloom until a week after Labor Day!

Anne, as usual, was undaunted. "But they last a really long time. They'll be in bloom until frost." And they did, and they were. Once they bloomed, they were quite lovely and gave the garden a great sunburst of color when everything else had faded.

In November I wheeled over the mower with the mulching plate in place and cut them down, pulverizing the plants and flowers. I should have worn a dust mask and overalls. The flowers were dry by this time, as was the dirt beneath them, and clouds of dust and seeds and pollen were flying everywhere. I finished the mowing and turned the remaining debris into the soil with the pitchfork before stumbling into the kitchen, dusty and coughing. And cranky.

"What happened to you?" Anne exclaimed.

"Sometimes I wonder why I do this," was all I could say as I headed to the bathroom for a long shower.

My back aching from turning in three hundred square feet of hard dirt, I dragged myself into work late the next morning, missing my own staff meeting. In the car, thinking about the garden as I often do, I remembered that

Bridget's blueprint had indicated a long row of marigolds along the stone wall. Anne and I had questioned her about it: Weren't marigolds annuals? We'd have to replant them every year.

"They are, but if you leave them in the ground, they self-seed incredibly well. You'll never get rid of them," Bridget had chirped enthusiastically.

We left them out of the garden anyway, since we had enough beds to keep us busy, but I thought of that conversation as I drove down the parkway. *They self-seed incredibly well.* Yikes. What had I been thinking? I had just turned literally thousands of marigold seeds into the corn bed! *You'll never get rid of them.*

I told Anne that evening that I had just planted a few thousand marigolds in the corn bed.

"In the marigold bed, you mean," she replied, unfazed.

Good point.

The experience almost made a weed revisionist out of me. The marigolds—flowers that I had purchased, planted, and nurtured—had now become weeds. I would have a similar experience in a few years when I tried a "wild" (as opposed to hybrid) arugula. This wild variety was, as promised, superior in taste to the hybrid. On a whim, I let just one plant overwinter and go to seed, and the next spring, the entire lettuce bed, two adjacent beds, and even the gravel paths were overrun with arugula. Is indeed one man's flower another man's weed?

What puzzles me about weeds is, Where on earth do

they all come from? It's a bit of a mystery to me. Lee Reich, in his book *Weedless Gardening,* implies that they don't necessarily *come* from anywhere; they are lurking in your soil all along: 140 seeds in every pound of soil, according to Reich, just lying dormant, waiting for exposure to light and air to sprout and dominate. That may be, but I think that the wind is at least an equal conspirator. I say this because I have observed shifting waves of weed attack over the years, in which a new weed will arrive in all my beds at the same time. I can remember the year purslane arrived as vividly as I do the arrival of my children. I had never seen this particular weed in my garden, and then one spring it showed up everywhere, and from all indications, it's here to stay.

Purslane, a common weed in much of the United States, is low growing and creeping. It has succulent leaves that distinguish it from just about every other weed in the garden. Purslane is incredibly tough to eradicate, partly because it seems to thrive everywhere: in dry soils, in moist soils, in sun or in shade. Most of all, it seems to like to come up under and wrap around my drip-irrigation hoses. I've observed that, remarkably, the roots take several forms, adapting to the conditions presented to them. Sometimes they are shallow and spread out; other times the plant puts out a long taproot that invariably snaps off and, Medusa-like, sprouts more plants before you can hang up your tools.

Purslane is impervious to hoeing, even if you manage to pull up the entire plant, unless you rake up (and, I suspect, burn) the debris. Left lying on the surface of the soil, the hoed-up plants reroot, like some science fiction monster that refuses to die. Thus purslane must be removed, plant by plant, with something like that horrible weeding fork my wife adores. In some summers it is responsible for 90 percent of my weeding time. In our garden it is the cockroach of the plant world. I suspect it will be around long after everyone and everything else is gone. I can't figure out why it hasn't taken over every square inch of soil in the United States. Maybe it has a weakness I haven't found yet.

It was after one of these brutal purslane-weeding sessions that I came in for a coffee break and saw there was an article about purslane in the *New York Times*—in, of all places, the Dining section. Remarkably, my nemesis was the latest trendy salad ingredient in New York's priciest restaurants. What a hoot: the thought of all these swells paying twelve dollars for a plate of weeds! I put down the paper, went back to the garden, and put a sprig of purslane in my mouth. Briefly. Yuck! Perhaps Le Cirque knows how to prepare it *just so*. But there was more. The article mentioned that the finest New York City restaurants were buying purslane from a small farmer who had converted his entire farm to purslane in—I couldn't believe it—the next town! Here I was, spending hours

No Such Thing as Organic Apples

It's not easy being green.
—Kermit the Frog

There's no such thing as organic apples in the Northeast," the local grizzled old farmer and orchardist told me. Although he would object to being called grizzled. And he's not that old. In fact, he's in his forties, has a college degree, and probably farms with the aid of a computer. Maybe that's why I didn't listen to him. Farmers have no credibility until they're old and grizzled. So I just nodded and pretended to agree, smugly secure in my knowledge that he was wrong. I had a plan.

The previous fall I had started a modest orchard—four apple and two peach trees. I had read the literature on organic fruit growing, I was familiar with IPM (integrated pest management), and like any respectable yuppie who came of age in the sixties, I was going to grow organic fruit and organic fruit only.

Commercial fruit, even if grown in town by your local

small farmer, is perhaps one of the two most pesticide- and fungicide-laden foods you will ever eat (the other one, by the way, is potatoes—but that's someone else's book). Environmentalists blame the farmers for overdosing with pesticides, and the farmers blame the consumers for demanding blemish-free fruit. Whoever is at fault, the result is that fruit trees are drenched weekly in enough poison to kill anything that happens to wander by—bad bugs such as maggots and codling moths, but also good bugs such as bees, lacewings, and ladybugs. With only six trees to tend, I figured I could pick off the bad bugs by hand, encourage the good bugs to stay, and, if needed, afford to use the more expensive "organic" fungicides and pesticides. *No,* I thought to myself as I listened to the nongrizzled farmer, *I will not produce poisoned apples in my backyard.*

My cockiness was based on more than simply the arrogance of the too highly educated who think they can learn everything from books; I did have some experience with organic farming. Growing up on suburban Long Island, in the shadows of New York City, I watched my father raise three apple trees that produced bumper crops of beautiful, perfect apples year after year. These were full-size trees, not the dwarf ones most popular today, and by the time I left home for college, these trees were the dominant feature—actually the *only* feature—of our small backyard.

As I recalled, this was my father's method of growing apples: On the first fifty-degree day in March, you fill your sprayer with a mixture of a few tablespoons of horti-

cultural oil diluted in a gallon of water. Then you pump
the handle, oh, about a hundred times until you feel as
though the next pump is going to send you, the sprayer,
and the orchard to kingdom come, lock the handle in
place, and press the trigger, coating the trees with the solution. Somehow, after about thirty seconds, the two thousand pounds of pressure you built up over ten minutes of
pumping is spent and your spray is reduced to a trickle.
Pump another hundred or thousand strokes, and repeat
until your trees are covered or you feel chest pains. This
"dormant oil" (thus named because you use it when the
tree is in its dormant stage) smothers any overwintering
insects or eggs, allowing you at least to head into spring
with a clean slate of pest-free trees.

This was, if memory serves, the only spraying Dad ever
did and the only attention he ever paid to the trees until
late spring, when the apples were the size of walnuts.
Then the whole family would gather in the yard, armed
with staplers, scissors, and rolls of clear plastic tubing
about three inches wide. Thus equipped, we spread out
among the trees, my dad taking a stepladder to reach the
upper branches, my little brother in charge of the lowest
branches, the rest of us in the middle. At each tiny apple,
we cut a four-inch length of tubing, slipped it over the apple, and secured it by stapling it closed at the stem.

Then the trees were ignored again until harvest. As the
apples grew, the plastic bags expanded with them, and by
October we were ready to pick large, unblemished (not to

mention prepackaged) fruit. The bags protected the apples from their most lethal enemy, the apple maggot fly, which lands on apples, lays about a zillion eggs, and flies off. These eggs hatch into the maggots that burrow into the apples and produce the characteristic deformed shapes and black dimples seen on untended trees. The bag is open on the bottom and top, allowing ventilation and growth, but the apple maggot fly apparently approaches the apples on a horizontal plane and deposits its eggs harmlessly on the plastic. It works.

One year, when Dad was unable to get tubing from his usual supplier, he made do with discarded small plastic bags, some of which had a company name printed on them. At harvest that year, in one of those great serendipitous moments in the annals of invention, he discovered that the label, by blocking the light and preventing the apple under it from turning red, had been clearly transferred to the apple. Bingo! A light clicked on in Dad's brain, and personalized apples were born. The following summer, Dad added a heavy black waterproof marking pen to the bagging arsenal. That fall (and every fall thereafter until his death in 1982), every member of the immediate family, as well as cousins, aunts, uncles, and selected friends, received an apple with his or her name on it. It was a sure sign of solid social standing with Dad if you received a customized apple, the local community's version of being invited to Truman Capote's Black and White Ball.

But why stop there? Dad moved on to apples with messages such as "Merry Christmas" while we kids winced and asked him, in vain, to put away the marker. Frankly I'm surprised that some commercial grower hasn't thought of this and produced apples with a trademark burned onto the fruit, or sold the space to Coca-Cola or NBC. Perhaps the cost of bagging would be prohibitive.

But of course, with a mere four trees, nothing is prohibitive. I wasn't sure about bagging (the aesthetics leave something to be desired), but I was sure I could produce organic apples in my backyard. I had planted bare-root trees—little more than twigs, in reality—from a mail-order supplier. I could have purchased larger, balled-root trees from a local nursery, but I would have been restricted to three or four of the most popular varieties—McIntosh, Red Delicious, maybe a Golden Delicious if I was lucky. In other words, the same boring apples I can buy in the supermarket for less than they cost to grow at home. That didn't hold much appeal for me. I was interested in raising so-called antique apples, the apples of our forefathers that are no longer widely commercially available.

Commercial growers (and others in the retail chain—distributors, shippers, and so forth) use a number of criteria in determining what kind of apples are grown and sold throughout the United States, but the number one consideration is handling. No matter what other positive attributes an apple (or a pear or peach) may have, if it doesn't store and ship well, you can't get it to market. If it bruises easily, if it gets mushy shortly after picking, it can't be shipped from Washington State to Florida.

A close second to handling is appearance. The apple industry is convinced that Americans don't want an apple that is uneven in color, russeted, or otherwise "unapplelike." The industry is banking on the fact that Americans buy fruit based on appearance, not on experience with taste or texture. As insulting as this sounds, the popularity of the Red Delicious apple supports the theory. By far the most popular apple in the United States, the Red Delicious looks absolutely gorgeous. And has virtually no taste, a mealy interior, and a tough skin. I cannot for the life of me understand why anyone buys or eats this apple. In contrast, the wonderful Granny Smith, a green apple popular in France, has only in recent years begun to make an appearance on American grocery shelves because distributors were sure Americans would never buy a green apple. The American public does seem to be slowly catching on, though. Red Delicious sales are down, Grannys are now widely available, and apple farmers are scrambling to replace their Red Delicious trees with other, more palatable varieties. So there is hope.

For myself, freed from the need to ship and sell my apples, I could grow apples that have fallen from corporate favor and the American consciousness. That meant buying trees by mail order. When my fruit-tree catalogs arrived in the dead of winter, I pored over them with a fervor most men reserve for Victoria's Secret. What tantalizing descriptions! What history! "The remarkable flavor has the barest hint of anise and is always deliciously spicy." "Goes back to Caesarean Rome." What variety! "The fruit is long and conical, yellow with red stripes." Surely the Yellow Newtown Pippen, "bred by the early colonists to satisfy British quality standards," and the oldest commercially grown native variety in the country, deserved to survive. Here's one I had to have: it is thought to have been planted by none other than Johnny Appleseed!

Johnny Appleseed? Isn't he an American *mythical* hero along the lines of Paul Bunyan and Pecos Bill? He is often thought of that way, but Johnny—born John Chapman in 1774—was an actual man, a serious man, a man with a vision. Chapman's vision, or perhaps his delusion, was an American frontier abloom with apple trees. The traditional view holds that Chapman, a devout Christian, envisioned sturdy log cabins built in orchards whose sweet blossoms inspired, and whose lush apples fed, the settlers as they conquered the wilderness. The less romantic historical perspective is that precious few of those apples found their way directly into settlers' stomachs. They were too valuable as the main ingredient for hard cider—apple*jack.* And it was apple*jack,* not apple *pie,* that fueled the homesteaders on the frontier. In any event, Johnny A. made enough money buying land and selling

apple seeds—that's right, selling, not giving away, seeds—
to become a moderately wealthy man (not that this eccentric ever spent any of it).

As Johnny made his way through the eastern United States planting orchards, he was also, perhaps unwittingly, performing a second important function: increasing the diversity of the species in America. Apples do not grow true from seed, meaning that if you plant a seed from a McIntosh apple, it will not grow into a "McIntosh tree," that is, a tree that yields McIntosh apples identical to those of the parent. If you want another McIntosh tree, you have to take a scion, or a cutting, from the fruiting portion of the tree and graft it onto a rootstock. Apples grown from seed will have characteristics different from the mother apple, sometimes wildly different. Most of the apples will be inferior, but once in a blue moon the offspring may be superior in taste or appearance, or have disease resistance, or keep longer, or have a faint banana smell or a striped skin. Note that Johnny wasn't grafting trees for forty-nine years. He was planting from sacks of seeds he lugged around the country. So he was single-handedly responsible for creating and spreading thousands of new apple varieties, ancestors of apples we still eat today.

One of the varieties rumored to have sprung from one of Johnny's seeds is the Grimes Golden, a native of West Virginia and a slightly spicy, juicy, golden apple thought to be an ancestor of the Golden Delicious. I decided this would be a good choice for our orchard. The other antique variety I selected, the Esopus Spitzenburg, was an easy choice. Not only was it first discovered in the Hudson Valley, just miles from our home, but it is also documented as having been the favorite apple of my boyhood hero, statesman-inventor-farmer Thomas Jefferson. Finally, to cover my bets (and on Anne's suggestion) I planted two trees of an outstanding modern variety, Empire. Developed in New York State, Empire is a derivative of the classic McIntosh, which it may well replace some day as a standard supermarket apple. Certainly it won the blind taste testing my family conducted during several trips to a local orchard. Zach, perhaps practicing for a future career as an oenophile, pronounced it "crispy, but not hard. Sweet, but not sugary. Hint of cider."

During these apple-picking and -tasting trips, we were able to sample over a half-dozen different varieties, including the newest disease-resistant ones. Logically, one would think the first step in planting an organic orchard should be to select disease-resistant varieties. But not surprisingly, we were disappointed in all of these apples because they are bred for resistance to blight, mildew, and scab—not for flavor. To us, they tasted bland and uninteresting, or, as Katie described one, "pukey."

Just *buying* apple trees required a bit of research and a number of careful choices. This is not like growing tomatoes or even peach trees, which are less challenging. The first thing to consider when choosing apple trees is that apple blossoms need to be cross-pollinated by a *different* apple variety in order to set fruit. This has several implications. The most obvious is that I needed to plant at least two types of trees. (Although one can buy trees that have two varieties of apples grafted onto a single trunk, this seems a touch Frankensteinian to me.) Less obvious is that the different varieties need to be in bloom *at the same time;* otherwise, no cross-pollination. Since some apples bloom later than others, one needs to know when the different varieties bloom. Fortunately this information is available in books and in some catalogs. Generally, if the apple ripens early, it blooms early as well. Some commercial orchards intersperse crab-apple trees among the others, as crabs tend to bloom early and hold their blossoms for a long time and thus make excellent pollinators. All four of my trees were listed as early- or mid-season bloomers, so I felt confident in having that base covered.

Another decision was how large I wanted the trees to grow. Years ago, there were only "standard" trees, full-size apple trees that grow to twenty or thirty feet in a great, spreading, twisting, gnarly growth. The Hudson Valley still has many existing eighty- or one-hundred-year-old specimens, twisted into fantastic, tortured shapes, providing the perfect backdrop for the headless horseman and frosty winter nights. But while stately and impressive, standard trees require a tall ladder for pruning, spraying, and picking, not to mention a good deal of space, and thus are less than practical for an amateur, even one with three acres of land.

I felt that a better choice was a dwarf or semidwarf tree, actually a "regular" tree grafted onto a dwarfing rootstock. As true dwarf trees generally have weak root systems and require staking, I went with semidwarf trees, which will grow to a quite manageable twelve to fifteen feet in height and can be kept ever shorter with pruning. Should you ever plant your own, be careful to look for the knobby graft at the base of the tree and make sure it remains *above* the soil when you plant. If you bury it, the trunk of the tree will send out roots above the graft, and you will—surprise, surprise—end up with a standard-size tree.

I did wonder how much fruit I was sacrificing by planting a smaller tree, but the answer was, remarkably little. Because semidwarfs set fruit more densely than standard trees and can be planted closer together (as close as ten feet), they actually provide a higher yield per square foot, which compensates for the reduced height. In fact, most commercial orchards are now planting exclusively semidwarf stock, which is not only more suitable to the popular pick-your-own type of operation that many orchards run, but also begins to produce fruit a couple of years sooner than standard trees.

That's right. I planted my trees in the fall, and it wasn't until two springs later that I had my first *blossoms*. That's also when I had my first problems.

Seemingly overnight, while I was sleeping, tent caterpillars netted out my apple trees and started munching on everything in sight. Everything, that is, except the remaining peach tree (the other had not made it through the first winter). Before I had noticed, the trees were nearly stripped bare. These critters put Agent Orange to shame. Panic-stricken, I consulted my organic-orchardist guide. Pick the caterpillars off by hand, then pinch them in half, it advised. Eww! But dutifully, after coming home from work, I changed from my dress shirt and tie into my grungiest slaughterhouse clothes and picked 'n' pinched until nary a critter was in sight. I was thoroughly nauseated, but they were gone.

For about twelve hours. The next morning, replacement troops had arrived and were happily munching away. Time to escalate. I stopped at a nursery on the way to the office and picked up a bottle of a spray labeled "organic," environmentally friendly pyrethrin soap. Pyrethrins are made from a particular species of African chrysanthemum that has developed a natural defense against pests. All right, better than a manufactured toxin that gets into the food chain and ends up wiping out bald eagles, I guess. But really, I wondered, how effective can a chrysanthemum be?

Very. This is amazing stuff. A spritz of pyrethrins on a caterpillar causes it to immediately curl up and fall to the ground.

Having narrowly escaped devastation by caterpillar, the apple trees grew new leaves and branches and all looked well until late July, when I noticed many of the leaves, especially on the antique trees, were turning brown and curling at the edges, giving the trees a wilted, sickly look. In fact, they appeared to be dying. I snipped off a twig and took it to my nurseryman, who took a quick glance at it and proclaimed, "Cedar-apple rust." Rust? My apple trees were rusting? It seems that cedar-apple rust is a fungus with a life cycle that depends on both cedar and apple trees. I went to the home-orchardist book for advice. Two solutions were offered: (1) remove any cedar trees within *two miles* ("Oh, Larry, sorry, my good man, but I had to chop down and burn all of your cedars today. Hope you don't mind"); or (2) use a friendly, natural organic spray of sulfur (listed as being "poorly effective") or a nasty chemical fungicide like Ferbam (listed as being "effective"). I looked at my sickly trees and figured a "poorly effective" treatment wasn't going to cut it.

Ferbam saved my trees that summer, but I felt guilty nonetheless, like I had taken the first step down a slippery (from toxins) slope. The following spring I was rewarded with a few blossoms and one Empire apple. I had raised an apple! I felt like Gregor Mendel. Encouraged by success, I hit the Ferbam early and often, watched the trees thicken and grow, and nurtured the single apple as if I were raising it for Eve. When it reached the size of a walnut, I dutifully cut a plastic sandwich bag down to size, slipped it over the apple, and watched and waited.

Through the summer, my little apple swelled and showed hints of red inside its protective sheath as my family waited in anticipation for the crisp fall day when, dressed in our L.L. Bean red-checked flannels, we would descend into the orchard and with great ceremony pluck the literal (and only) fruit of our labors.

But before that day could arrive, on a sweltering mid-August afternoon, I bumped the tree slightly with the lawn mower, and the young apple, bag and all, plopped unceremoniously to the ground with a muffled thud. From Gregor Mendel to Homer Simpson. I sheepishly brought it inside to face the silent stares of my inquisitors. "Must be ripe. Popped right off," I said cheerfully. We sliced it into quarters and ate it on the spot. It was the best apple I have ever tasted, if a bit tart. And hard.

But I was heartened that summer, not discouraged. I had proved to myself that I could indeed grow, if not organic, at least pesticide-free apples. True, I'd had to resort to a manufactured fungicide to save the trees from the rust, so I'd lost my "organic" badge of honor, but at least I had avoided introducing to the orchard a manufactured pesticide that kills bees and butterflies and birds. And now, as fall stiffened into winter, the branches were swollen with buds and the promise of a full crop in the spring.

The winter that followed was a remarkably mild one in the Northeast. February temperatures soared into the eighties as daffodils bloomed. By March, an entire month early, two of the trees were in full bloom, a merry explosion of pink and white popcorn. I could almost see the blossoms unfurl right before my eyes, as if watching a time-lapse nature movie. I had never seen such a lovely sight. I walked daily among the trees and marveled at the flowers, my flowers. Even if only half of them produced fruit, I would have bushels of apples. Bushels of Empire apples. Yep, both of the trees in bloom were Empires.

And that's when it hit me. My focus moved to what *wasn't* blooming—either of the antique trees. Still recovering from their brush with cedar-apple rust, they had few buds, and the ones they did have didn't look as though they'd be opening anytime soon. In other words, I had nothing to cross-fertilize my Empire blossoms! But wait, Larry had planted McIntosh trees last year. I checked them out: no buds at all.

Something else was missing, too. Where were the bees? It was only March. Perhaps they were still asleep. Or was this a symptom of a larger problem? Bees have been in general decline over the past several years, a decline blamed on pesticide use and a destructive mite that has been depleting the population. Perhaps, like frogs, bees are a natural barometer of our environmental health. If so, stormy times are ahead. Whatever the reason, this year there was nary a bee in sight.

So, no complementary blossoms and no bees. Terrific. I was going to have to take matters into my own hands if I was going to have more than ornamental trees this year. The research institute where I work at my day job (which I will not be giving up for a farmer's life anytime soon) is located on the grounds of a state psychiatric hospital built in the 1920s. Outside the former director's mansion stand rows of old, stately apple trees. They make quite a sight, their weathered, contorted limbs spiraling up into spreading canopies. And in early March they, too, were in bloom. I didn't know what variety they were, but given their age, they couldn't possibly be Empire. So at lunch I tucked my necktie into my pants, went out with pruners and a plastic garbage bag, and snipped off dozens of blossom-laden twigs. Fortunately, no guards came by; just a couple of cars slowed as drivers peered over quizzically. "Just needs some pruning," I shouted as I snipped.

At home I pinched off the pollen-bearing stamens into a mortar and ground them up with a pestle to release the pollen. Then, borrowing a small artist's paintbrush from my daughter, I flitted from tree to tree, humming "Flight of the Bumblebee," dipping the brush into the mortar, then deep into each blossom, doing Mother Nature's work for her. Now I *really* felt like Mendel.

In the kitchen, which overlooks the orchard, Anne handled damage control.

"Why is Daddy painting the apple trees?" Katie wanted to know.

"He's pollinating the trees, honey."

"What does that mean?"

Zach passed through on his way to the refrigerator. "No birds-and-bees talk in front of me, okay?"

Birds and bees, indeed. By the time I was done, I felt strangely, strongly aroused. That night, the smell of pollen still fresh in my nostrils, I made passionate, urgent love to my mystified (but appreciative) wife.

Two weeks later, many of the blossoms had been replaced by tiny, embryonic apples. Dozens and dozens of them. It had worked! Victory was within my grasp. Time to lay on some Ferbam and start collecting plastic bags.

Well before the apples were ready for bags, when they were the size of cherries, it was clear that I had another problem. And as with the caterpillars the previous year, it seemingly happened overnight. Nearly every apple was dotted with black pockmarks. I pinched a few off and split them open with my fingernail. The black marks on the surface were the openings of black tunnels that wound through the interior of the apples. Something—most likely apple maggots—had infected nine out of every ten apples. I was sick. I slumped down on the lawn and tried to understand what I was doing wrong. This wasn't like growing apples in the shadows of New York City. I was slowly starting to realize that Dad hadn't had to deal with the various fungi, insects, and rusts that are prevalent wherever you find orchards and farms—and the Hudson Valley has plenty of both.

I went back to my books on integrated pest management. The underlying principle behind IPM is the avoidance of prophylactic, wide-spectrum spraying. "Wait until you have a problem, identify the pest, and then treat that specific pest," goes the credo. With a touch of sadness, I sprayed the trees with the recommended chemical insecticide. Another step down the slippery slope: I was no longer organic, I was no longer even insecticide free. I *was* practicing IPM, at least, but in the end, IPM was, for me, a dismal failure. Perhaps because I wasn't using indicator traps, perhaps because I didn't have the time to spend on tree inspection, the insecticide came too late to save the infected fruit, which littered the ground in May. The dozens and dozens of blossoms that had held so much promise in March ended up yielding a handful of fruit—not even enough for a pie.

The flaw in IPM for the home orchardist, it seems to me, is that unless you have the luxury of being able to inspect your trees (or traps) every twelve hours, by the time you see a symptom or a pest, it is too late to treat it. Things happen quickly in the orchard, and pesticides applied to the outside of an apple do not reach the insect or eggs already inside. And now, having compromised my organic principles, in using both fungicide and insecticide on my trees, I didn't even have any apples to show for it.

I discussed this with Anne. "We don't practice medicine this way," she said.

"Practice what way?"

"It seems like you're waiting for the symptoms to appear before you treat the disease that you *know* is coming. Preventive medicine is much more effective. You need to prevent the disease from developing in the first place."

"You don't spray your patients with malathion."

"No, but we give them vaccinations. And we prophy-lactically treat high-risk patients with medication or ad-vise behavior changes to prevent the disease from getting a foothold." She paused. "And your apples are high-risk patients."

She had that right.

Over the winter, as new buds again swelled with the promise of fruit, I agonized over my next move. I had seen two potential bearing years of apples go to waste; the scorecard read "Pests 2, Me 0." I needed a win.

One thing was certain: I was going to have to resort to at least some prophylactic spraying next year. But I wasn't ready to throw in the organic towel yet. I picked up a can of "earth-friendly fruit-tree spray." In addition to my fa-vorite African chrysanthemum, it contained rotenone, an-other naturally occurring pesticide extracted from the stems and roots of a few tropical plants. But the mix con-sisted mainly of copper and sulfur—two elements found in nature, to be sure, but not ones I normally sprinkle on my food. I started applying it regularly in the spring, every two weeks.

We had a more conventional spring that year, the trees all bloomed in April at about the same time, when the bees were awake, and it became clear—again, before bagging time—that I had fungus and insect problems. That was enough. I had tried, I had really tried, but I was coming to the inescapable conclusion that chemical spraying was unavoidable if you wanted an edible apple crop—not a *perfect* apple, but just an *edible* apple. I would have been quite happy to harvest pockmarked apples that proudly brandished the "organic" label, but this was not one of the options. My only choices seemed to be no apples or nonorganic apples.

I started to question my stubborn adherence to "earth friendly" chemicals and organic solutions. What is "organic," after all? Is a chemical from an African chrysanthemum that is so powerful it makes a caterpillar shrivel up and die within two seconds really "earth friendly"? Is strychnine (an "organic" poison extracted from the seeds of the imaginatively named *Strychnos nux-vomica* tree) "better" than malathion (extracted from the laboratories of Drexel Chemical)? I'd rather have malathion on my food. This is not to minimize the impact on humans and the environment of manufactured pesticides, but in the microcosm of my orchard, I was beginning to acknowledge that I had a choice. And if my only choices were to feed my family commercial apples or apples that I had raised, even if they were sprayed with chemicals, wouldn't the latter be far preferable? At least I would know what was on them, and how much.

This was a painful conversation for me to have with myself. Not only was I still trying to live up to the exemplar of my father's organic apple orchard, but I am a natural-fibers, NPR-supporting, recycling, compost-making, left-of-center environmentalist, and I put my money where my mouth is, supporting local groups like Scenic Hudson to clean our rivers and curb development. Yet I was an environmentalist with a problem: I wanted to grow apples.

So when the serpent offered me the pesticide-sprayed apple . . . I accepted it.

But the fall from innocence was not yet complete. That didn't happen until, opening the bottle of Agway wide-spectrum orchard spray, I was startled by a distinctive, familiar smell. You know how a certain smell can, through some miracle of brain chemistry, transport you back to a place and time, awakening a lost memory? That's what happened when I opened the orchard spray. But these madeleines transported me back to the *pesticide* of my youth! I knew that smell! Damn it, I grew up with that smell! Could it be? Could I have so romanticized my father's "organic" apple raising that I had wiped out any conscious memory of pesticides? Or had he perhaps sneaked in a little malathion now and then when I wasn't looking?

I was at once shocked, confused, and disillusioned. And most of all, no longer innocent. I had been chasing an ideal that didn't even exist. The shackles gone, I started to laugh, in relief perhaps, but mainly at the joke. I don't think I had ever before laughed while working on the apple trees. It had been mostly worry and disappointment. But we laughed that day, Dad and I, for a long time, in the basement, mixing orchard spray. Because in the Northeast, you see, there's no such thing as organic apples.

You May Be Smarter, But He's Got More Time

DEER DIES AFTER CROSSING MANHATTAN ROADWAY

A deer that had apparently been wandering around Washington Heights in Manhattan died yesterday after being struck as it crossed morning traffic along the Henry Hudson Parkway, the police said.

—The New York Times

ELECTRONIC SINGING FISH DRIVES DEER FROM GARDEN

Dear Heloise,
After trying many chemical potions to scare deer away—with lukewarm success—I hit on the idea to use one of those motion-activated singing fish to scare the critters away . . . It works great for me and requires virtually no attention after mounting on a stake in your garden.

—Hints from Heloise

The din of Big Machinery had long faded to the two-note song of chickadees, but the kitchen garden was not yet complete: it needed a fence. A very effective fence. I faced this task reluctantly. The garden looked so beautiful in its present (defenseless) condition, sitting just beyond an old stone wall, that I didn't want a fence to spoil the pleasure of viewing it. I also wasn't looking forward to the inevitable and interminable battle to come, a defensive battle, no less. The worst kind. Every good man would prefer offense to defense. I am speaking, of course, of the age-old war of man (and his garden) versus beast.

Never in the history of the North American continent has the deck been more stacked in favor of the beasts. Here in the Northeast, as in many parts of the country, herds of deer roam through neighborhoods unmolested while the kids who used to roam through the neighborhood now sail through cyberspace. Groundhogs build underground networks that put the New York subway system to shame. And just when you've finally secured the perimeter, birds swoop down from the skies.

Before discussing the sometimes grisly details of this battle, I should point out, in the spirit of full disclosure, that I have historically had a poor rapport with animals, *all* animals: domesticated, wild, just about any kind but grilled.

I attribute this to having spent my formative years in suburban New York (emphasis on the *urban*), where, surprisingly, no one in my neighborhood had any pets (unless you count little Debbie Sparhuber, who, for the briefest of times, had a salamander—or perhaps it was a newt—in a mayonnaise jar). During my entire childhood, the only mammals we ever saw in the neighborhood were stray dogs or an occasional raccoon, the latter being a nocturnal animal that you are not supposed to see during the day, unless, of course, it is rabid, a lesson that was constantly drummed into my malleable young head by parents, grandparents, aunts, and uncles, whose biggest fear, apparently, in moving from the relative security of Brooklyn (!) to the wild suburbs of Long Island was rabid animals. Consequently I emerged from my childhood having learned the lesson that animals not in a museum or on your plate were animals to be feared.

And the animals know it. Dogs take one look at me and growl. Cats pee. I have never been horseback riding without receiving a condescending scolding from the trail master—"Horses can smell fear"—as Trigger lurches off in the wrong direction.

We have had no better luck with pets, either. When Katie was eight, we bought her a dog and returned it after one of the most traumatic twenty-four hours of our lives. We eventually replaced the dog with a less demanding rabbit. He died in a month. Then we tried an aquarium, which is about as far down in the animal kingdom as you can get while still claiming to own a "pet." Even that proved too much of a challenge. One day while cleaning the tank, I accidentally turned the heater knob all the way to the right and literally cooked all the fish.

I felt a little more comfortable setting out to deal with animals in the garden, for the strategy there centered on keeping animals out of my life, not in it. And so far, keeping animals out of my life was something I'd rather excelled at.

As construction of our garden neared completion, I had to decide on what type of fencing we would put up. Not putting in fencing was never an option. Because of that lovely old stone wall that ran the length of the garden, I did not want to do anything to detract from its aesthetic. Yet the low wall itself did not pose enough of a barrier to do the job. We considered a four-foot fence built atop the stone wall (yuck) and a fence just inside the wall (better, but not much) and finally settled on using a few strands of electric wire, which is fairly inconspicuous, above the wall. A couple of wrought iron gates (insulated from the electricity) gave us access. I had at this point been using an electric fence more or less successfully to protect the orchard, so I already owned the expensive components (mainly the charger), which made this option especially attractive.

An electric fence is usually used to keep livestock in, but it can also be effective at keeping wildlife out. The high-quality models originate from either New Zealand (developed for the huge sheep-farming industry) or

Germany (don't ask). The American ones that Agway-type stores sell are reputed to be junk. The charger is basically a giant capacitor that builds up and discharges a six-thousand- to ten-thousand-volt charge about once a second. Because the amperage is low, and the duration brief, the shock is not harmful to humans or wildlife, but it does give a pretty good zing.

Ask our tree surgeon. A year after wiring the orchard, we contracted to have a large, diseased tree taken down about seventy-five feet from the fence.

I called Cory, the local tree surgeon, and started to give directions.

"Not the Big Brown House!" he said. "I know the place."

Naturally.

Cory lives up to his occupation's odd title. He could drop a hundred-foot oak between the two yellow lines on a highway. Cory is impossible not to like, one of those tall, lean guys, all sinew and muscle, but the kind of muscle that comes from honest climbing and tree rassling, not the unnatural bulk and bulging biceps of a weight lifter. He has three assets that make him ideally suited to his job: First, he is somewhat shy and more comfortable a hundred feet up in a tree than talking with clients. In fact, his business card not-so-subtly proclaims (after "Over 18,000 dangerous trees taken down safely"), "Happiness is to be alone when we work." Second, he can scamper up a tree like a monkey. No cherry picker for him, thank you.

He straps on his crampons, and up he goes. Third, and most important, for our part of the country, he is one of those fortunate people with complete immunity to poison ivy. He can (and often does) wade through it all day long with no ill effect, whereas if I even see it, I start to itch.

So one Saturday, Cory arrived to tackle this huge white oak, hard as rock, a hundred feet tall and four feet across. To get a controlled fall in the right direction, he had set up a guy wire, a strong wire with a ratchet on one end, between the tree and his truck. Unfortunately the guy wire ran from the truck, through the orchard, passing directly on top of an electric wire, and then to the tree. Apparently Cory had not seen the yellow WARNING: ELECTRIC FENCE sign sitting in my workshop, which I hadn't quite gotten around to hanging yet. He started to ratchet up the wire, and *zap!* He fell back, shook his head with a "What the hell?" daze, and grabbed the ratchet again. *Zap.* "Jesus!" He then concluded that (1) he was receiving an electric shock, and (2) his truck's electrical system was the source. Sometimes half-right is worse than not right at all. Determined to find the source, he hopped up to his pickup truck, which of course was now electrified to the tune of six thousand volts. Every second. *Zap* one thousand, *zap* one thousand, *zap* one thousand.

Finally Zach tore himself away from the window and the strange dance he was witnessing and called, "Mom, did Dad remember to turn the fence off?" Cory, ever the good sport, did not walk off the job and did not sue me. I was mortified, but he was just relieved that his truck didn't have an electrical problem.

Reasonable people may wonder why I had a six-thousand-volt electric fence around my orchard.

PICTURE A COUNTRY WHERE herds of two-hundred-pound animals roam freely among the peasants. The animals destroy all of the peasants' gardens, eat their food, and defecate on their lawns. The animals also carry disease: one particularly nasty disease that can be difficult to diagnose and debilitating if not treated. These animals also injure and occasionally kill the peasants. The peasants complain but take no action. The government does nothing except continue to enforce policies that ensure the continued propagation and health of this species. If a peasant tries to kill one of these beasts himself, he will be arrested.

What country would tolerate this, placing the welfare of the animals over that of its citizens? Why, the United States, of course. The animal in question is the white-tailed deer, *Odocoileus virginianus,* and the disease is Lyme. Nationwide, according to the Insurance Institute for Highway Safety, there were 1.5 million deer crashes in 2003, resulting in $1.1 billion in vehicle damage and a startling 161 deaths. Not to mention up to $76 million in commercial crop damage in New York State alone. This is remarkable: 161 people *killed* in collisions with deer and undoubtedly thousands of deer killed by cars, and this mutual slaughter doesn't even make the news!

Lyme disease is caused by a bacterium found in infected deer ticks. In its adult stage, the tick's preferred host is the white-tailed deer, which provides not only transportation for the immobile tick but a blood meal for the female's three thousand eggs. In 2002, over 23,700 cases of Lyme disease were officially reported nationwide by the Centers for Disease Control (90 percent of that in the Northeast), meaning the actual number is likely several times higher. And yet, one eighty-five-year-old man dies of West Nile virus, and state and local governments shift into panic mode, blanketing the region with tons of insecticides with no prior discussion of policy, study of efficacy, or analysis of safety. Go figure.

My theory is that no one takes Lyme disease seriously because it's named after the quaint little town in Connecticut where it was first discovered, while West Nile virus sounds exotically Nubian, excitingly dangerous, and, most of all, very, very foreign. So despite the fact that it had only killed a handful of people, and that they were nearly all very elderly people who were going to die from whatever illness they got next, be it a common cold or West Nile virus, New York treated it like the return of the Black Death.

Which is why I scan the morning newspaper every day, hoping for, praying for, news of a deer carrying West Nile virus. Lacking such a discovery, it seems that Bambi and

family are here to stay for a while, because the government seems totally stymied. Just why is a bit of a mystery,
since this is not, after all, a seemingly unsolvable problem on the scale of the Middle East conflict, world hunger,
or AIDS. This is *deer*. Deer that typically do not, during
their lifetimes, roam more than a mile from where they
were born. This fact alone would seem to narrow the problem down to a simple reduction or elimination of a contained population of deer, and the town would not have to
be overly concerned about deer from other areas moving
in to fill the void. To make the solution even simpler, the
deer have gotten so tame (or so bold) that you can approach them very closely. Or to put it less delicately, you
don't have to wait to shoot until you see the whites of their
eyes. Why, Marshal Dillon, I reckon a team of sharpshooters could clean up this town in a couple of days and make
it safe for the God-fearing good people again. Who could
possibly object to such a simple and effective plan? Just
about everyone in my town, that's who. These are some of
the arguments I hear:

The deer were here first. Nonsense. The deer population on the East Coast of the United States is an order of
magnitude greater than when the Pilgrims landed. The
deer were not here first; we have created an ideal environment for them with our azaleas and lawns, while consid-
erately removing all of their natural enemies. Except one.
And that one is only allowed to hunt them for a couple of

weeks out of the year, and only in designated areas, and is restricted by a host of regulations.

Oh, they're so cute. The flowers that used to be in the spot now occupied by stubs and deer turds were cuter.

People and deer can coexist if people will plant deer-resistant plants. Take my word for it, there is no such thing. Not in my neighborhood, at least. And even if there were, why should we be restricted to growing only 1 percent of the available plants just to accommodate this oversize rodent?

I don't want guns being fired in my neighborhood. I admit, it takes some getting used to, but towns have brought in professional sharpshooters for several days and reduced the herd with no public accidents.

We need to keep the deer population up for the hunters. This argument is only heard from the hunters. The ethics of hunting aside, this is a bogus line of reasoning. The nearest hunting preserve is miles from most suburban towns. The deer in my neighborhood have never set foot on hunting ground and never will. Unless, of course, we bring the hunters to them. But there is a larger problem here. Deer management in New York comes under control of the New York State Department of Environmental Conservation, which still views these vermin as a resource to be carefully managed and protected, not as a pest. The state strictly regulates how many deer can be taken (especially females), requires hunters to drag each one to an official station to be weighed and inspected, and keeps detailed statistics on the annual take and population. This is all for the benefit of the hunters, so that, God forbid, the poor weekend hunters (who on any given day are mistakenly shooting more cows, dogs, and people than actual deer) won't have to go home empty handed.

It's just wrong. And of course there are many who feel just plain uneasy about slaughtering animals — and stripped to its essence, that's just what I'm proposing. These people fall into two camps: animal-rights proponents and everyone else. There is no point in even trying to discuss this with the animal-rights people (except to say that if they would divert just half the energy they spend on animal suffering to reduce human suffering, the world would be a far better place). To the others, I say I sympathize. I feel uneasy about it, too, but would suggest they open their eyes and think about how the chicken, beef, pork, and fish they are eating got on their plate. If we find a better, more humane way to reduce the deer population, I'll be all for it, but in the meantime, the rifle is all we have.

With no hope that anything would be done about this problem anytime soon, I was left to defend my own turf. This was complicated by the fact that Larry next door started feeding the deer a few years after we'd moved in. He said he did it to lure them into eating the deer food, rather than his shrubs, but in my opinion this only resulted in attracting many more deer than we had before he opened his buffet. Deer aren't stupid; when food is around, word spreads. They may eat his feed instead of his shrubs for dinner, but they're having my garden for dessert on the way home.

Then, as if that weren't bad enough, new neighbors moved in on the other side of us and announced their plans to put up a salt lick for the deer, leaving me—and my garden—stuck in the middle between two feed troughs.

Clearly the neighborhood was not sympathetic to my cause. I would have to buttress my defenses.

The first volley of the Battle of Bambi was lobbed when I planted the small orchard: half a dozen apple and peach saplings, not much more than twigs really, with young, tender shoots. Without a fence of some sort, the orchard would be no more than a snack bar for deer. I decided to construct the electric fence.

For deer, which can jump a seven-foot fence, a short and permeable electric fence functions as a psychological barrier, since the deer, if they choose, can easily jump over or between the wires. Nevertheless, for the first few seasons my fence was about 90 percent effective—not perfect, but boasting a higher rate of success than any psychiatrist I know of.

When I first constructed the orchard fence, I used only two strands of a thin, slightly stretchy wire rope, placed about two and three feet above the ground, and a highly visible half-inch plastic-and-wire tape for the top strand, at five feet. I dabbed the tape at intervals with peanut butter. The goal is to train the deer that this fence—and what lies beyond—represents pain. Their fur, particularly in winter, is such an effective electrical insulator that brushing against the fence may not give enough of a shock for deterrence, but contact with the lip is another matter. Later, once word had gotten around the local herd that the orchard was off limits, I replaced the somewhat obnoxious-looking tape with another strand of wire.

And word does get around, or so it seems. One good shock to the mouth or nose seems to deter not only the victim but the entire clan for weeks. That suggests that there is at least some communication between deer, or perhaps they always follow the leader. Occasionally a deer will wander in. This most often happens in winter when a dry, heavy snowfall prevents the earth from serving as the electrical ground, rendering the fence less effective. Inevitably the deer, which somehow entered the orchard painlessly, gets zapped and turned back on the way out, eventually choosing to bolt through the wires, snapping them in the process. But the wire is easily patched, and the deer returns to his family with a horror story bound to keep all of them away for a while. Every so often I will go around with strips of aluminum foil and a jar of peanut butter to counter a new incursion. During one particularly bad winter, I watched the huge animals splay their legs and, incredibly, squeeze in under the bottom strand, white-tailed calypso dancers. So I added another, lower strand and some fresh peanut butter.

And so it goes. They get in, you buttress the fence, and

they stay out for a while. They get back in, and you bait and buttress some more. With the deer pressure increasing dramatically, whether because of my neighbors' game-farm mentality or just because the herd is growing in size, the electric fence has been proving less effective over time. Recently the fence was shorted out for two weeks while we were away on vacation, and the deer not only ate everything to the ground but kept stubbornly coming in, jumping between the wires, even after I had repaired the short and baited every few feet, the psychological barrier having been broken. Feeling a bit like a circus trainer, I switched to a different bait and covered the electric fence with a seven-foot mesh to provide a physical barrier until the psychological one could again be established. Eventually we may end up installing a tall mesh fence around the entire yard, but that seems such a drastic step that we keep putting it off.

WHEN BUILDING THE FENCE for the kitchen garden, I had to contend not only with deer but with an even bigger threat, the groundhog, aka woodchuck. Groundhogs are like deer in that they have thick, dense fur that is an effective insulator against shock. Groundhogs, often more of a nuisance in the garden than the white-tailed deer, are so destructive and so difficult to deter that they have been known to drive gardeners to give up their gardens altogether. To keep the groundhogs *and* the deer out of the kitchen garden, I built a fence similar to the orchard's, with the addition of two low wires for groundhog deterrence. I ran those wires alternating positive and ground so as not to have to rely on moist earth for a good ground. Deer may jump, but a groundhog will dig *under* a fence to get into your garden. Conventional wisdom holds that surface fences don't work; the rule of thumb is that the bottom of your fence has to be buried eighteen to twenty-four inches underground. Try finding a fencing contractor to do *that* job.

But oddly enough, the groundhog does not attempt to burrow under an electric fence. Perhaps the shock is enough of a deterrent to dissuade it from persistence. Or perhaps the way the groundhog passes under a conventional fence is by feeling its way down underground until it finds the end of the fence, or tires of digging, somewhere around the eighteen- to twenty-four-inch mark. Obviously it would not want to feel its way along an electric wire pulsing six thousand volts every second.

Conventional wisdom also states that an electric wire at two inches and another at twelve inches is sufficient to deter a groundhog. And for years it was, until I met the groundhog I named Superchuck.

Superchuck and I should never have crossed paths. In a sense, I created Superchuck. Ever since I had replaced the broken concrete slab in our little barn with a raised wood floor (when I converted it to a woodshop), the nether land of the barn had been home to groundhogs, skunks, and even foxes. But mainly a series of groundhogs. Other

than the fact that they smell up the barn, they weren't both-
ering me any, so I had been letting them be. Until the day
a voice startled me as I was coming out of the woodshop.

"Those groundhogs are going to cause you trouble," the
voice chanted.

"Hi, Larry. Nah, I don't think so."

"You want to borrow my trap?"

Larry let me know he had just chased a groundhog out
of his garden and watched it scamper under the barn—
my barn.

That made me an accomplice. So to be a good neighbor,
and also because I'm no fan of groundhogs (not to mention
that it would be nice to be free of that odor), I started con-
tinually trapping and releasing them miles away on state
property. But groundhog homes are apparently like Upper
West Side apartments. Word travels quickly when one is
free, and within weeks, a new groundhog has moved in.
(No, it's not the old one returned through some Incredible
Journey. Trust me.)

Eventually I would realize that by constantly removing
easy-to-trap groundhogs, I had created my own little Dar-
winian universe. Each time I got rid of another dumb, easily trapped one, a replacement soon moved in. But a
smart, wily one would avoid the trap and find a way into
my garden. In other words, the groundhogs I trapped and
removed were precisely the ones I should have been keeping under the barn. They were the ideal tenants!

But this nuance didn't register with me until much

later. So I kept trapping and replacing groundhogs until, inevitably—Darwinianly—I found Superchuck living under the barn.

I first heard about Superchuck before I saw him. Anne told me a groundhog was eating the tomatoes. I had so much faith in my fencing that I was a little skeptical at first. I picked a blade of grass and touched it to the fence. Ouch. The fence was working.

"Maybe a large bird," I suggested.

"Then we better keep the kids inside until you capture it. Look at the size of this bite," Anne said, displaying a tomato with a huge chunk missing.

It did look like a groundhog bite. Then visual confirmation: over the next few weeks, we occasionally saw him lounging and eating in our garden. I hauled out a Havahart trap, baited it with apples, and set it in the garden. No luck, of course. After all, why would he go into a little cage for food, when he has the entire bounty of the garden spread before him? For several days we observed him eating, sunning, and just generally hanging out in the garden like Brigitte Bardot on the Riviera. I never saw him enter, but when startled, he dashed between the electric wires as if they weren't there. I spent a morning adding a few more strands of wire close to the ground. My wires were now about three inches apart. There was no way he could slip between them without getting shocked. Nevertheless, the next day, there he was again, munching on the lettuce.

This didn't make sense. I checked the voltage on the

fence. Only three thousand volts. It should have been registering at least six thousand. Ha! A rational explanation! His thick fur was insulating him from the "mere" three-thousand-volt current. After the fence company's technical people walked me through some tests, they determined that my charger was bad. Rather than repair it (and be without it for a week), I opted to buy a new, more powerful one with a ten-thousand-volt charge.

"Can I ask you a question?" Anne said, noting the escalation into five-digit voltage. "Is this safe?"

Now, that was an interesting question. The catalog naturally insisted that fences were safe for humans, but it did include a disturbing disclaimer. There was indeed, out of the thousands of chargers and fences they had sold, a single case of a human fatality. I told Anne the story as she blanched.

At this point I would have put up a fence with a *hundred* thousand volts if that's what it took to protect my Brandywine tomatoes, so I forged ahead and phoned in the order. The new charger arrived in the mail two days and a half-dozen tomatoes later. I hooked it up and waited for the remaining tomatoes to ripen.

As did Superchuck. He was coming into and going out of the garden so frequently now that it wasn't uncommon to see him penetrating the fence as I watched from my kitchen window. Once, I actually saw him crawl through, jerking violently from a shock, and continue on. He was willing to absorb a ten-thousand-volt shock to get a tomato! This was not supposed to happen. The whole idea of an electric fence is deterrence—pain— and it is based on the science that animals do not like shocks. But Superchuck had figured out that the shock wasn't going to kill him, and after all, I *was* growing heirloom Brandywines.

At least he had good taste. Brandywine tomatoes are one of the best-tasting tomatoes in the world and are nearly impossible to find at farm stands. The Brandywine was first introduced by Amish farmers in 1885 but has only become well known to gardeners and gourmands in the past decade or so. I think they would be more widely sold were it not for the fact that they are prone to cracking near the stem, a visual defect only, but as with apples, a near-fatal one in our image-obsessed society.

The cracking didn't bother Superchuck, who preferred the Brandywines to the cherry and French tomatoes. A few days later, there he was again, in the garden. I was starting to develop a kind of respect for this fat, ugly, Brandywine-loving groundhog who was rewriting the book on pest control. I should have captured him for science, but I was in a war, and losing. In order to maximize the voltage, I went out and bought some four-foot-long galvanized steel grounding rods and pounded them deep into the earth to get a better earth contact for the ground wires. I ran more wire between the other strands. I smeared the whole thing with peanut butter. Still he continued to raid the tomatoes. Then one day, in what seemed like a rare moment of lucidity, I put the trap, baited with cut-up apples, *outside* the fence, hoping that he would tire of the shock and go for the easy meal in the Havahart. I set the trap up in the morning, before going to work. That evening, there was nothing but browned apples in the trap. Now, you really shouldn't leave the trap loaded overnight, because you might catch a skunk or some other nocturnal animal, but Superchuck was an early riser—much earlier than I—so I left it loaded with the browned apples and went to bed.

The next morning, as I made coffee, a movement outside the window caught my eye. The trap! Victory! I wanted to release him as soon as possible before Houdini could work an escape.

"Zach, would you put the cage in the back of the wagon, please?"

Zach grumbled, rubbed the sleep from his eyes, and shuffled out the kitchen door. A moment later he reappeared, panting and white as a sheet, slamming the door behind him as if being hotly pursued. I was alarmed.

"Zach, what's the matter? Are you all right?"

His eyes were as big as apples.

"Dad, that's no groundhog," he panted.

"Then what is it?"

He mutely shook his head from side to side.

I decided I'd better go out and have a look. Clearly I

wasn't going to get any useful information out of my squeamish son. "Really," I muttered, "I've got to do a better job of introducing these kids to nature."

A moment later I was back in the kitchen, panting and white as a sheet.

As I had approached the trap, before I was within six feet, a snarling, tooth-baring, drooling opossum had started leaping for my jugular. I had never been close to an opossum, but I had trapped squirrels and groundhogs, and I had never been afraid of an animal in the trap. Until that moment. An opossum is one nasty animal, with a long, tapered tail, sharp, pointy teeth, and really, really unpleasant eyes. And this one was clearly not happy with me.

If you've never had the pleasure of using a Havahart, the way you release the animal is by approaching the door end of the trap. The animal generally retreats to the opposite end, and you release the latch, open the door, and poke a stick through to keep it open. Not until you walk away will the frightened animal venture out. At least, that's the way it had always worked with groundhogs, squirrels, and birds. But it didn't look like the possum understood the rules, and this time *I* was the frightened animal.

I explained the situation to Anne.

"What are you going to do?" she asked.

"It hasn't been doing us any harm. I guess we really should just release it." I considered the unwelcome prospect of returning to the trap. "How much do you love me?" I ventured.

"Oh, no. I'm not going anywhere near that thing. He's your pet."

So I swallowed my fear, grabbed a stick, and approached the trap. The snarling, tooth-baring, drooling opossum from hell, instead of retreating to the other end, started snapping at me, the cage rattling violently and inching closer with each leap. Frankly I was terrified and returned to the kitchen.

"What if he's rabid?" I asked Anne. "I mean, he's acting really weirdly. I'm getting freaked out."

"Foaming at the mouth?"

I wiped my mouth with the back of my hand.

"Not you, *him*. Is the possum foaming at the mouth?"

"I think he's drooling. Maybe I'll just let him sit for a while and calm down."

"You both need to calm down," Anne said, patting me on the back as she left the room.

Midday, I approached again, with the same result. Neither of us was showing signs of calming down anytime soon. I returned to the kitchen, where the family had gathered for lunch.

"Dad, what are you going to do with the possum?" Katie asked.

There was a long, silent moment during which I felt the collective stare. I had already decided what I was going to do; I was just stuck figuring out how to explain it. For during my walk back to the kitchen, I had examined my conscience, weighed my options, and decided simply to leave him in the trap for a few more hours, leaving him to die of dehydration. This may sound heartless, but on a hot day, which this was, an animal in the trap will usually die fairly quickly, within a couple of hours. In fact I've accidentally lost a couple of groundhogs that way, and I always feel a little bad when it happens, but it seemed preferable to getting attacked by a possibly rabid opossum.

"I think he's going to"—I searched for a word that I could slip past a child without upsetting her—"expire in a few hours."

"Dad, that's horrible! You can't murder him!"

Zach countered, "Katie, he tried to kill me! He's evil!"

"You can't just let him die."

This wasn't going well. I had an idea. "Katie, why don't you go take a look at him. See how he's doing."

Katie went outside, we heard a rattle from the cage, and she came back a minute later and went straight up to her room without a word, her eyes wide. I now had unanimous, if silent, consent.

Except that at sundown, ole possum was still alive and kicking.

The next morning, though, it was motionless, thank goodness. Until I approached the trap. Then the snarling, tooth-baring, drooling opossum from hell starting snapping at me again. I left it for another day and night. The following morning, I approached the trap again. The snarling, tooth-baring, drooling opossum from hell took another shot at me, but by this time its heart clearly wasn't in it. Then again, neither was mine. We were now into day three. I can tolerate killing an animal, especially one presenting a danger to me, but I am not into torture, and this was starting to feel like torture. Not to mention bad karma. That phrase kept popping into my head like a mantra: *Bad karma. Bad karma.* I was still afraid, though, and opening the trap did not seem like a good idea. Yet I had to put this creature out of its misery. I had created this cruel situation, and now a quick, merciful death seemed the best of my bad options. I had once read the most humane way to kill a small animal in a trap is to attach a rope to the trap and fling the whole thing into a pond. In lieu of a pond, I filled the largest garbage can I had with water and dumped the trap in.

The opossum, instead of drowning, climbed to the top of the cage, which was just sticking out of the water, and starting eagerly lapping up the water. Instead of drowning it, I was reviving it! This was no opossum, this was Rasputin. All right, enough! My courage inspired by the snarling, tooth-baring, drooling opossum from hell who refused to die, I threw the cage into the car, drove to the state lands, said a quick prayer, and opened the trap door. Ole possum, wet, exhausted, half-drowned, and half-dead, scampered out and ran—more like stumbled—into the woods, to what fate I knew not.

And the bad karma? The very next day, the temperature set a record high. We don't have air-conditioning in our house but instead depend on a house fan set into the attic floor. It sucks air in the windows and sends it out the attic vents. I arrived home from work and switched on the house fan. Nothing. I couldn't believe it: hottest day of the year, and the house fan decided to break. So up into the attic I went. God, it was hot in there; it must have been at least 140. Hot, dry heat that stung my lungs when I inhaled. As I worked on the fan, once again lamenting my mechanical ineptitude, sweat dripped off my face like a steady rain. I started feeling a little light headed, the attic started feeling like a dream, and gradually it dawned on me that I was becoming dehydrated. For two days that poor possum sweltered in the heat. *So this is what it's like,* I thought. And that instant I knew with absolute certainty that possum was dead, that it had stumbled into the woods to die, the victim of my torture.

Now, if this were a Stephen King novel, the attic door would accidentally shut and lock, the family would be out, and I would expire in the attic.

This is not a Stephen King novel. I got out of the attic, downed a few glasses of ice water, and, miraculously, a new fan belt from an automotive-parts store solved the problem. But I was spooked for days.

In the meantime, I still had a masochistic woodchuck absorbing his daily near electrocution and eating his way through my harvest. Understandably the experience with the opossum had damped my enthusiasm for the Havahart (which I renamed the Havahartattack), so I refocused my attentions on making the garden impenetrable. I added wires, I moved wires, I changed connectors, I redid my ground rods, I tried to squeeze every last volt out of the charger. Still it wasn't enough. Superchuck, undaunted by my efforts, and now with that pesky possum out of the way, continued to visit the garden and raid the lettuce and tomatoes.

"I think we need more volts," I ventured to Anne.

She muttered something semiunintelligible, which may have been along the lines of "You need more brain cells."

I didn't pursue it. More voltage wouldn't have helped, as I was about to learn. For one day as I watched through the window, I saw a remarkable thing: after chowing down in the garden, Superchuck, ready to hit the lair under the barn for a good nap, slowly approached the fence, then paused just in front of it, crouched as if waiting for just the right moment, and timed a leap through the wires, easily passing through in the second between pulses. He had learned how to avoid the shock! Now, this was remarkable. This truly was no ordinary groundhog.

But I was no ordinary gardener. And now it was getting personal. I was not about to be outsmarted by a groundhog. This guy had to go. I broached the idea of buying a rifle with Anne. No dice.

"What about a BB gun?" she suggested.

Just the kind of response you'd expect from a woman. "What the hell am I going to do with a BB gun?"

"Shoot the groundhog," she said in a tone that suggested she meant, "Shoot the groundhog, *dummy.*"

"You can't kill a groundhog with a BB gun. You might scare it, but a groundhog that isn't afraid of ten thousand volts isn't going to be deterred by a Red Ryder."

"Well, no rifles in this house," she said, ending the conversation. I would remind her of this exchange with delight in a few years, when the deer had become such a nuisance that sweet Anne would advocate annihilation by rifle, arrow, or plastique. But for now, no guns in the house.

It seemed as if the thing to do was to evict the tenant. Convert his tunnel into a living tomb. Seal him off. I read on the Internet (so it must be true) that if you fill the main exit, plus the two or three escape routes they typically have, with a sixty-pound bag of cement, groundhogs will asphyxiate before they can dig a new exit. I had located two escape routes Superchuck had dug outside the barn; the problem was that the main opening was somewhere in the crawl space under the barn. There was not enough room for a human to squeeze through, so the only way to seal off all escapes would be to first seal off the barn with a two-foot-deep underground fence around its perimeter, then seal off the other escape exits with cement before he knew what was happening. This looked like three to five back-breaking days of work, and there were two ways it could turn out, neither one particularly attractive: First, it might not work (I could miss an escape route, or the Internet author may be full of beans). The second possibility, that it might indeed work, would leave at least one groundhog (and maybe a whole family) dead and stinking directly under the floor of my woodshop. I abandoned the idea.

Frankly, I was out of creative ideas, so once again I hauled out the Havahartattack, determined not to leave it baited at night, and this time I placed it not in or near the garden but right outside the barn, where it would be the first thing Superchuck saw when he came out for a snack. And instead of apples, I threw in a couple of nice, ripe Brandywines.

And miracle of miracles, the day I set the trap, another blistering August day, I came home from work to find Superchuck's huge frame crammed into the trap. Dead. I was almost sad. He was a worthy opponent, crafty, innovative, and determined. And I, I was just . . . lucky. There was no thrill of victory, only a sense of relief. I dug a grave in the woods on my property. As I was throwing shovelfuls of dirt on Superchuck, I had a momentary scare—I thought he twitched, and I panicked: *Oh, no, now what do I do? I'm burying an animal alive! Do I have to bludgeon him with the shovel? My life is becoming one endless Edgar Allan Poe tale!* But I guess it was just rigor mortis setting in, or his body shifting in the grave. He never moved again.

Predictably, a new groundhog showed up under the barn within a couple of weeks. I've been letting him be.

THE ONLY ANIMAL I have seen that is more persistent than a groundhog is a squirrel. One summer day, we had some guests over for lunch. As we were sitting on our porch overlooking the orchard and admiring the serenity of a perfect summer afternoon, we saw a squirrel hop into the orchard, scamper up a tree, bite off a golf-ball-size apple, and scamper away. Cute. Our suburban guests were very amused by this quaint display of country life. Five minutes later they were amused again. And five minutes later, again. And so on, like clockwork. They were hysterical. I was beside myself. I did a little math in my head: 12 apples an hour times, say, five hours a day equals 60 apples a day, equals 420 apples a week. If this kept up at even half the pace we were witnessing, the orchard would be cleaned out in a week.

I'd had my trees for several years at this point and had never seen squirrels stealing the crop before. But the past spring and summer had been devastatingly dry. Farmers without irrigation had no crops. Towns had instituted water restrictions. I surmised that the squirrel was using the apples as a source of water.

But what to do? He might have been ready to pick the apples, but I sure wasn't; they were still a good few weeks from maturity. I needed to get to the Agway, and fast. We were on dessert. Surely our visitors would be leaving soon.

Anne offered seconds of peach pie.

"No thanks!" I practically yelled before anyone else could answer. "Too rich!"

Anne glared at me.

"I could sit here all afternoon," said one guest, sighing,

as Anne brought more pie. I almost choked. "And this pie is fantastic. But we'll have to get going soon." That was more like it. They had stopped by on their way upstate and still had a two-hour trip ahead of them.

"How much of a drive do you figure we have from here?"

Anne started to answer, "No more than two—"

"Four hours," I interrupted.

Our guests exchanged a look.

"At least," I added as I watched the squirrel out of the corner of my eye. "Traffic, you know." From behind the visitors, Anne grimaced and made a slashing motion across her throat, which I took to mean either "Cut it out," or "I'm going to kill you when this is over."

Our guests were still waving from their car as I hopped in mine and sped down to the Agway. I told my tale to the pest expert there.

"You don't say!" he declared. "I've never heard of that. Hey, Rich! " He called over another salesman. "You got to hear this." I had to repeat the story to Rich, which cost me at least two more apples. He asked where I lived. I started to describe the place.

"Not the Big Brown House!" he exclaimed. "You still have sheep?"

"Sheep?"

"Yeah, Kreske kept sheep so he could classify it as a farm. Cut his property taxes in half. And he didn't have to cut the grass."

Or fertilize, I imagine. This was a story I'd have to come back for, but minutes were passing and apples disappearing. I got Rich back to the problem at hand, and we mulled over the options. There was pepper spray. ("But I've got to eat the apples, too," I reminded them. They assured me it came off with soap and water.) We considered bird netting, but a net large enough to drape over an entire tree with enough left to secure at the base cost fifty dollars, and I had four trees to cover. Two hundred dollars would buy a lot of apples at the farm stand. I couldn't bring myself to spend two hundred dollars to try (and possibly fail) to protect trees with no more than fifty dollars' worth of apples on them, so I left with the pepper spray for ten bucks. This stuff was supposed to be hot: "Keep from face and eyes," the bottle cautioned. I drenched the apples in pepper spray.

Apparently the squirrel had watched me from afar, for the moment I left the orchard, he bounded in, grabbed a Mexicali apple in his mouth, and bounded off to eat it, or bury it, or whatever the hell he was doing with them. And five minutes later, he was back. And so on. Maybe he was making salsa.

THE EXPERIENCE BROUGHT BACK bad memories of my first battle with squirrels, years ago in our first house in Yonkers. We had purchased the house through an estate sale. The owner had passed away over a year earlier (we seem to have a habit of buying abandoned homes), and we were the first suckers to offer anything near the asking price over the course of a year. Our offer was accepted so quickly that we wanted to rescind it. ("Oh, did I say a hundred and *ninety* thousand? I meant a hundred and *nineteen* thousand. I always get those two mixed up.") But as I've mentioned, it was a fine house, and we loved it, cracked plaster and all.

So did a pair of squirrels we came to call Chip and Dale. On our very first morning—*very* early morning— we learned two things without leaving our bed: (1) the New York State Thruway was a *lot* closer than we realized: we could hear the trucks shifting gears in the predawn; and (2) we were not alone. The pitter-patter of little feet directly overhead was our first clue that Chip and Dale were well established in the attic and, for all I knew (assuming that unlike their Disney namesakes, Dale was a female), planning on starting a family. Time to evict.

I settled on an absolutely foolproof strategic approach. First I found where I thought they were getting in and out: a small gap in a valley on the roof. I brought in plaster and chicken wire but did not seal the hole up yet. I wanted to catch and remove the squirrels and *then* quickly seal up the opening. I bought my first Havahart trap (the "squirrel model"), baited it with peanuts, and waited. And waited. A week later, we were still waking to the sound of highway and squirrels.

And then, one Saturday morning, we awoke to a new sound: the rattle of a cage. Victory! This was the first creature I had ever trapped, and I hadn't yet learned to drive it two counties away, so I took it to a small park a few blocks away and released it. Back at the house, I inspected the attic. Empty. This is what I had hoped for and expected, for we rarely heard the squirrels during the middle of the day, when I presume they were out gathering nuts or stealing apples. I worked the chicken wire into the gap, slathered the whole thing in plaster, and opened a beer. Well, that wasn't so bad.

Sunday morning, we woke to the sounds of eighteen-wheeler transmissions . . . and pitter-patter above our heads. We still had a squirrel in the attic. I'll venture a guess and say it was Dale. Why? Because I heard another sound: the sound of a squirrel scratching on glass. I went outside and looked up. Chip, the gallant fellow, had found his way back from the park (probably before I had) and was desperately trying to rescue Dale. Now, it's quite possible I have this backward, but because I was raised on notions of classical chivalry, I'm going to stick to the assumption that the female was stuck inside, and the male was trying to claw his way back in. And he didn't work on the glass for long. He soon moved to the window frame itself and started to *eat his way through it*. Now, this was truly alarming. We had owned this house less than two weeks, and a lovesick squirrel was eating it up. It was interesting that he had chosen the frame to break through, not some other weak point in the roof (and I'm sure there were plenty). Did he choose the window because he could see his beloved on the other side as he gnawed? Years later it seems quite touching, actually, and I wish I could have reunited them, but at the time it was nothing short of terrifying. We were afraid to open the front door, for fear he would shoot through and make for the attic. It was like living Hitchcock's *The Birds,* only with squirrels.

I set up the trap in the attic again, now in a race against time. Dale, however, was lying low. Each day, meanwhile, Chip got a little farther into the frame as I watched helplessly. *So this is home ownership,* I thought ruefully. I wanted to call the landlord, to yell at the super. But they were both me.

Eventually, after a few tense days, Dale got hungry enough to overcome her reservations and ventured into the trap. I released her far, far away, and the instant she was removed, Chip stopped gnawing. I examined the frame. He was only another day from breaking through, and I faced a considerable repair job. Amazing.

The most valuable lesson I learned from this experience came not from the squirrels but from a work colleague, a thoughtful Irishman with wire-rimmed glasses and a snow-white mane and beard. Jim is only a hundred pounds removed from being Santa Claus. My co-workers during this period were receiving daily updates on Squirrel Wars, much to their delight. Most of them considered it all a real hoot, some demonstrating their sympathy and wit by whistling the *Rocky and Bullwinkle* theme each time I passed them in the hall. On the day that Chip was within a half inch of reaching Dale, I sat in Jim's office, despondent, looking for an answer. Jim listened to me for a while, stroking his beard thoughtfully and staring at the ceiling.

"The problem is," he finally said, pushing his glasses up on his nose, "you may be smarter, but he's got more time."

Truer words were never spoken.

AFTER WATCHING MY CURRENT peppery-apple-loving squirrel make a couple of more raids on my apples, I couldn't stand it anymore. I settled on a compromise solution: netting two of the trees and preemptively picking all the apples off the others. We made several apple pies with the tiny, tart apples. Then, predictably, the squirrel got hung up in the netting. I was able to untangle him without harm to either man or beast, and I guess he learned his lesson, because on his next trip back he chose to go for the apples in—believe it or not—the Havahart. I took him far, far away, but I know he—or his kin—will be back.

Nature Abhors a Meadow
(But Loves a Good Fire)

We did it with a plan that seemed valid and workable. Things happened that we couldn't or didn't anticipate.

—Roy Weaver, Bandelier National
Monument superintendent

With the kitchen garden established, I decided—in an act of horticultural hubris perhaps not seen since, well, since Yahweh designed the Garden of Eden—to Build a Meadow. This ambition was fed by my sixth viewing of *The Sound of Music,* with its breathtaking opening scene of Julie Andrews twirling around in the Alpine field of grasses and wildflowers (including, of course, edelweiss), followed by a trip of ours to a remote section of Prince Edward Island. Our rental cottage was perched on a seaside bluff next to a lighthouse in the most marvelous meadow I have ever seen. The relentless ocean wind kept the grasses short and thin, and the field was speckled with wildflowers of a half-dozen varieties, with nary a weed in sight. One of my prized possessions to this day is a photograph of Katie walking through this seaside meadow, the flowers up to her knees, the lighthouse shining proud in the background.

As it so happened, our property had a large area that had been cleared of brush as part of the installation of a swimming pool. I decided it would make an ideal meadow. So with Julie singing and dancing in my head, and egged on (almost criminally) by glossy wildflower-seed catalogs, I set out to Build a Meadow.

Getting wildflowers to grow in a bare patch of earth is easy. After all, that's why they're called *wild*flowers. The trick to maintaining a meadow is to keep the even wilder flowers—that is, weeds—from moving in and taking over. But how to do this in a large meadow? If I relied on the stirrup hoe, I'd end up making Millet's *Man with a Hoe* look like *Man on Vacation* by comparison. Mulching wouldn't do, either, as it would suppress the spread of the very plants I was trying to grow. In a meadow, one ends up in a delicate balancing act: the field needs to be wild, but not *too* wild. When it comes to gardens (if not life), absolutes are easy; balances are tricky. It's not so hard to maintain a weed-free monolithic lawn of Kentucky bluegrass, with its underground runners and thick carpet of growth. Environmentally unsound, no doubt, as this usually involves the application of tons of chemicals and water, but when it comes down to it, relatively straightforward.

But to turn that lawn into a diverse ecological environment requires more skill and effort.

So how does one create a meadow? Well, if you take a cue from nature and travel to the western prairies or an Alpine (or Prince Edward Island) meadow, you'll find that a meadow is actually made up mostly not of flowers, but of grasses — wild, native grasses. In North America, these might be big or little bluestem, switchgrass, or Indian grass, to name the more common types. One characteristic these native grasses share is that they are "bunch" grasses that do not spread by underground runners. Rather, they grow in clumps, allowing the wildflowers to come in between them and take up the bare spots before weeds can get established. Grasses such as Kentucky bluegrass or (in the South) Bermuda grass, which spread via underground runners, would eventually choke out the wildflowers, and in a few years you'd be left with just another lawn to mow and fertilize and water.

A couple of seasons earlier, I had tried to grow some native big and little bluestem grasses in another part of the yard, with no success whatsoever. In fact, my pound of bluestem seeds, for which I paid some hugely exorbitant price, yielded exactly *one plant*. That is a ratio of failure to success of something like ten thousand to one, a ratio even I couldn't tolerate, so when I designed the meadow, I ditched the idea of using a true native grass and instead selected perennial rye. It may not be traditional, but it seemed as though it would accomplish the same goal as any of the true prairie grasses. The weeds wouldn't know the difference.

The wildflower-seed catalog I was consulting (note to self: use catalogs for buying, not as sources of information) advertised a number of "clay buster" wildflowers — that is, flowers that will not only tolerate clay soil but send out deep roots that loosen and break up the clay. This was of particular interest to me because my meadow site was nearly solid clay. In fact it had a foot-deep topdressing of the brick-quality clay that had formerly resided in what was now the bottom of our pool. This material (I won't dignify it by calling it soil), which came from eight feet under, should never have seen the light of day, but there it was, spread out on top of my Hudson Valley topsoil — dull gray brown, nonporous, and, depending on the weather, either baked and hard as rock, or wet and slimy enough for the weekly mud-wrestling match at Fantasies.

My catalog promised to turn this barren landscape into a joyous meadow (Julie not included, although there were plenty of photographs of little children prancing about). I eagerly ordered not envelopes but pounds of flower seeds — echinacea, daisies, and black-eyed Susans — and on a late-September morning, I mixed them all together in a bucket with some ryegrass and raked and sowed and raked some more, then went up to the house and waited, like an expectant father, for spring.

In March the winter snows melted, and I held my breath

through several April storms that I feared would wash the seed down the slope, but by summer it became apparent, somewhat to my surprise, that I had indeed built a meadow. Now, I do have to qualify the word *meadow*. What I had at that point was a lot of small, stubby plants that had germinated from seed, but not, that first summer, a lot of flowers. That was to be expected. Perennial wildflowers spend their first year sending roots down and getting established; then they start growing upward and worry about reproducing. (If you failed high school biology, this is where the flower comes in.) But I was certainly on the right track, and here and there a precocious flower even bloomed.

The following summer, it actually looked like the meadow of my dreams. By June the field was sparkling with hundreds of white daisies, and by July the black-eyed Susans showed up, although the echinacea (purple coneflowers) never busted through the clay, except for a stray here and there. One other little glitch became apparent that summer. I thought the daisies I had selected would bloom through the summer, like black-eyed Susans and coneflowers, but I had chosen the wrong variety. These daisies vanished around the Fourth of July—just about the time we start using the adjacent pool, which overlooks the meadow. Oh, well. I still had the black-eyed Susans through the summer, and the important thing was, I had Built a Meadow! I felt a little like God, Zeus, and Martha Stewart all rolled into one.

I was a little surprised by how high the ryegrass grew.

I was hoping it would top out at about two feet, more or less the same height as the flowers, but it kept zooming up and by July was hiding many of the flowers below it. The grass had to be cut. But how? Certainly not, at three feet tall, with a mower. I had always been fascinated with scything, and I like anything that doesn't require an engine, so, still caught up in my *Sound of Music* fantasy, I ordered a Swiss scythe by mail. I figured a few swings with that baby a couple of times a year would keep rye down and Susan up while providing me with some exercise. It even looked as though it would be a fairly enjoyable activity, swinging this glimmering steel blade to and fro while walking through my meadow, singing, *The hills are alive . . .*

I used it once. Half an hour later, back aching, with a lot of dented ryegrass, I stowed it back in the basement, where it still hangs, waiting for a more skilled (or patient) operator.

In addition to being tall, the ryegrass also seemed to be spreading. As in, *invasively.* Maybe it wasn't spreading by underground rhizomes, but it was nevertheless spreading. It was slowly starting to take over the lower meadow, squeezing out the flowers.

Meanwhile, the upper, wetter part of the meadow had already lost a battle to quackgrass, that tall, wide-bladed grass that loves wet soil. Because of the new clay "topsoil" that had been spread throughout, the drainage patterns of my yard had been changed dramatically, with a wet, marshy area forming in the margin between end of lawn and beginning of meadow. The quackgrass and the rye were battling for turf, with the shrinking "meadow" caught in the middle. In the midst of it all, bull thistle, a nightmarish tall weed with spiked leaves so sharp they will penetrate cowhide gloves, was moving in. It was time for action.

It is not unusual for man-made meadows to require maintenance. Just as man-made beaches need constant infusions of new sand, if you are going to try to imitate nature, you can't just do it once and forget about it. You have to keep at it. This is the lesson the U.S. Forest Service is (slowly) learning in managing our vast forests and trying to prevent them from becoming tinderboxes. And the formula for maintaining meadows and "domesticated" forests is remarkably similar: managed fires.

In the case of the meadow, the current thinking is that one should set the field ablaze every spring or so. The fire, naturally, doesn't discriminate and burns everything to the ground, killing the annual weeds and any weed seeds in the vicinity. The wildflowers and natives grasses are burned to the ground as well, but the deep roots of the grasses and wildflowers survive the burning and, now with plenty of light and air, send up new growth and prosper. This annual burning is meant to mimic the action of natural, fire-starting lightning storms in the great prairies (which we generally don't get in my backyard in the Hudson Valley), in the same way that managed forest fires are meant to reverse the consequences of years of aggressive firefighting of naturally started blazes in our national forests.

The day *Building Controlled Fires* arrived in the mail, Anne looked a little worried.

"What's this for, dear?" she asked, her voice slightly higher pitched than normal.

I gave my best James Stewart impression. "Time to burn the prairie, darlin'."

"You're joking, right?" she said.

Uh, actually, no. Fire was a bit of a sore spot between us because I had nearly set the house ablaze the previous January. On a frigid winter night with the temperature dropping below zero and the north winds pouring through every crack in our stone foundation—and there are plenty—the water pipes supplying the kitchen had frozen solid. I spent the next morning in the basement with a hair dryer crammed up between the stone foundation and the kitchen floor, trying to thaw out the pipes, but cold air was coming in as fast as I could warm it, and I was getting impatient.

"This is a toy. Time to get a real tool," I said to myself as I headed down to the shop to retrieve my electric paint stripper. "Now we're cookin'," I muttered as I placed the nozzle up against the pipe. Anything hot enough to melt away six layers of paint and make floor tiles peel up in agony ought to be able to melt a little ice in a copper pipe.

Holding the paint gun soon got tiresome, however, so I

locked the trigger in place, propped the gun in the crevice with a brick, and sat down in a lawn chair to leaf through some garden catalogs. Sometime later, I heard yells from the kitchen above.

"There's smoke pouring out of the dishwasher!" Anne cried.

I jumped out of the chair. Oh, my God, the floor joist was on fire! This timber had had ninety years to dry out, and it was burning like fatwood. There was no water faucet in the basement. "Send Zach down with a pot of water!" I yelled up through the floor. The next few minutes remain a bit of a haze for me, but with water and rags I managed to extinguish the fire—but not the memory of my recklessness.

Patience in thawing out pipes is a good thing. (I must try to remember that.)

So Anne was understandably not enthusiastic about the prospect of using fire as a gardening tool. "I don't want to know any more," she wisely concluded, and left me with my book.

I have to confess, I was also a little squeamish about setting my yard on fire, but I had been building bonfires (outdoors) for a couple of years by then, and that experience, along with the genetic memories passed from my caveman ancestors, had left me somewhat confident in my ability to control fire. I had been building bonfires because, when our septic field had finally been completed, I had asked the backhoe driver to rip out some tangly brush before he left. (I had to get *something* out of storing that damn backhoe in my yard for six months.) By the time he was done, he had accumulated quite a sizable pile of grape and other miscellaneous shrubs and vines. Could he cart it away? I asked.

"I can't do that," he said. "Dumping fees are ridiculous."

I looked dolefully at the huge mound of brush. "What am I going to do with it?" It was too tangly and voluminous for the chipper.

He looked at the two acres of woods behind him. "Want me to haul it back there?"

I really didn't. Two acres may seem like a lot of space, but if you start dumping yard debris out there, it fills up quickly. We didn't want our woods to look like a dump. I shook my head.

"Why don't you just burn it?" he suggested.

"Burn it?" Having grown up in a suburban town where the fire department would come calling if your barbecue was too smoky, this seemed unthinkable to me. "How?" I asked stupidly.

He patiently explained the process to me. I simply had to get a permit from the town clerk, call the fire and police dispatcher when I was ready to start (so they would know to ignore all the 911 calls they were sure to get), then start a small fire with kerosene—not gasoline—and small branches. Once it caught, drag the big stuff onto the pile, and open a beer.

I thought it sounded dangerous.

"Nah," the excavator assured me. "It's easy. Just keep a hose nearby, and don't leave it unattended. You have good water pressure?"

I nodded.

"And the fire department is only a half mile away if you get into trouble."

He ought to know. I found out some months later that I had been advised to build a huge, sixteen-hour bonfire in my yard by none other than the town fire chief.

I have since given up this filthy, somewhat antisocial habit of burning my brush, but as I say, I was a veteran of several fires by the time I was contemplating setting fire to the meadow. I resolved to burn it that spring, after we had returned from a family Easter vacation in the Southwest.

Even though this was early April, the garden was, as always, a family member that had to be accommodated. I had eight trays of young seedlings growing under fluorescent lights on the enclosed porch, and they wouldn't survive the nearly two weeks without water. After considering several options, we decided to bring them to Anne's office, where one of her staff had offered to tend them.

Near the end of our trip, we visited Bandelier National Monument, an hour or so from Santa Fe and adjacent to Los Alamos, home of the nation's worst-kept nuclear secrets. Hidden in the Jemez Mountains and only rediscovered in 1880, Bandelier is a magical place, once the home of the Anasazi Indians, who dug scores of cliff houses in the soft volcanic walls and erected large, multistory pueblo dwellings in the valley. One can still climb rickety wooden ladders and enter the cave dwellings, their ceilings black from the soot of cooking fires. For hundreds of years, the Anasazi lived in the valley, farming, hunting, fishing, and taking water from the stream that flowed year-round through the floor of the valley.

Then around five hundred years ago the Anasazi cliff dwellers left their valley and cave dwellings behind and vanished, virtually without a trace. A number of theories have been proffered to explain their sudden disappearance from the Jemez Mountains and other settlements in present-day New Mexico, ranging from the mundane (climatic change) to the exotic (ritual cannibalism). Granted, I'm no archaeologist or anthropologist, but having visited a few of these sites, I lean toward the mundane. As I wandered through these settlements, I found myself asking, not why they left, but why they came. It looked as though it must have been a difficult, on-the-edge existence in a dry, hostile environment. Perhaps my theory betrays my avocation, but when it comes to Bandelier, at least, I wonder if the explanation may simply be that the stream dried up. The stream, the sole source of water for drinking, farming, cooking, their very lifeblood, dried up, and they had to move on. For while you may be able to carry sufficient water into that valley for drinking and cooking, you cannot carry enough in for irrigation, for farming. In other words, the farmer in me thinks they left simply because they couldn't farm.

As we approached Bandelier that day, we were greeted by the disturbing, acrid smell of smoke. Then as we entered the park, we drove past the smoke and, alarmingly, orange flames of brushfires. It was a startling sight. Right alongside the road, the forest was gently but steadily burning, small orange flames licking at the bases of the pines, feeding on brush and fallen needles. Being easterners, our first reaction was, "Jesus Christ, the forest is on fire! Run, Thumper, run!" But a park ranger explained that we were witnessing a so-called prescribed burn set by the Parks Service to rid the forest floor of dangerous, combustible brush and debris that, if left in place, would someday inevitably feed a huge, uncontrolled fire. We were relieved by the news, and the strategy seemed to make sense, but still, we all agreed, it was a tad spooky that there was no one around the fire we had witnessed. Shouldn't someone be standing there watching it, attending it? I remembered what the town fire chief had told me about standing by with a hose.

By the time we stepped off the plane in New York a couple of days later, the smoke was choking Santa Fe, the laboratories and secrets of Los Alamos had been abandoned, and the Bandelier fire, wildly out of control, was front-page news even in New York. Before the fire was extinguished some days later, it had destroyed 260 homes, forced the evacuation of 25,000 people, and destroyed

48,000 acres of New Mexico (but not, thankfully, the priceless ruins of the Anasazi).

Roy Weaver, the Bandelier superintendent who gave the go-ahead to light the match, later said, "I don't want to deny our responsibility for igniting the prescribed fire. But we did it with a plan that seemed valid and workable. Things happened that we couldn't or didn't anticipate. And that we couldn't control."

WE RETURNED HOME to eight trays of withered seedlings. A total, heartbreaking loss.

I thought about my meadow. And hubris. And about my well-thought-out plan that also seemed valid and workable. I wondered what the things were that I couldn't anticipate, and of course I knew that I couldn't anticipate the things I couldn't anticipate. I gazed at my weedy meadow and pictured it ablaze. Suddenly the prospect seemed chilling. I pictured myself being interviewed by the local paper, my neighborhood, my *town* a smoldering ruin, saying, "But I did it with a plan that seemed valid and workable. Things happened that I couldn't or didn't anticipate. And that I couldn't control."

So today my copy of *Building Controlled Fires* sits collecting dust on my bookshelf, having assumed the role of a curious relic, not a well-thumbed how-to guide.

The meadow is reaching middle age now. It has forgotten my plan for it and is becoming what it wants to be, as is nature's wont. And it wants to be tall—very tall—ryegrass with a scattering of daisies and black-eyed Susans that are visible for a few weeks of the year. I've given up trying to maintain it, for the most part. Some purple loosestrife moved in a few years ago. I let this invasive nonnative live for a month or so, enjoying its splash of tall violet among the rye, then ripped it out before it could go to seed and start taking over. I mostly just let the meadow be, but once in a while I give it a little help.

I suppose if nature had wanted a meadow in my yard, she would have put one there long before I had the idea. A perfect meadow, such as the one on Prince Edward Island, is there because conditions at that location are perfect for a meadow. The strong ocean winds that keep the grasses short, the absence of weed spores blowing in from the ocean, the well-drained soil, other factors beyond my vision—these natural features have all come together in this spot to build a perfect meadow.

Yes, with enough determination, you can build and maintain a meadow anywhere, a beautiful *Sound of Music* meadow. But you need lots of time, a strong back, and the nerve—or hubris—to light the match.

And here is something else I've figured out: I don't have the time, I never had the back, and thank you, Mr. Weaver, for teaching me a thing or two about hubris.

Shell-Shocked:
A Return to the Front (Burner)

For the tree is known by its fruit.
—Matthew 12:33

"Can someone go out and get me some thyme?" I asked as dinner hour was approaching. Not an unusual request, yet Anne pretended not to hear me, Katie pulled her sweater up over her face, and Zach spoke for all when he said, "Have fun with that, Dad."

I grabbed my parka and a trowel. It was February, we were in the middle of a blizzard, and the thyme in the garden was buried under a winter's worth of snow. In other words, it was the perfect night for a piping hot potato-apple-thyme gratin.

Since we have all that thyme obscuring the spigots, I always have some available—enough to operate a small green market, probably. Thyme, *fresh* thyme, is a marvelous herb. It's the secret (along with one slice of candied ginger) to my chicken soup, great in marinades, and capable of transforming boring eggs into one terrific *omelette aux fines herbes.* Its tiny leaves can be quickly stripped from the plant by drawing thumb and forefinger down each twig, against the grain, right into the food, without dicing. Additionally, this underappreciated herb keeps its leaves—and its flavor—right through winter, especially if protected under a thick blanket of snow.

I trudged toward the garden, almost leaving my boots behind in a snowdrift, and pushed on the iron gate. It wouldn't budge through the deep snow, so, turning off the electric fence, I slipped between the wires for the short jump from the stone wall into the garden, landing softly in a white pillow. In the dusk, the garden had taken on that eerie bluish hue you only see on winter evenings and, despite the snow, felt restful and quiet.

And mysterious. The snow had blown and drifted so much that it was difficult to distinguish the paths from the beds. The garden was a blue gray arctic wilderness, an unbroken two-dimensional landscape of undulating snow interrupted only by the sundial and several trellises. It was breathtaking. I paused for a moment to admire its beauty, to absorb its stoic patience with the storm that had been making me antsy. A slap of wind-driven snow to my face snapped me back to my mission. It looked as though it would be easier to find my old septic tank than to locate the thyme.

As I was trying to visualize the garden beneath its thick white quilt, something ten, fifteen feet away caught my eye, just barely peeking out through the snow, waving to me in the wind. I approached it. No, it couldn't be, that would be too lucky . . . wait, it was . . . thyme! Using my trowel, I cleared the snow away and pinched off a few sprigs. That was easy. *Sometimes I get to win one,* I thought, straightening up to find myself facing Larry, sitting high in his Jeep, staring at me over the hedge. I triumphantly held up and waved the thyme at him so that he wouldn't think I was totally nuts. Without responding, he engaged the snowplow mounted on his Jeep and zoomed up his driveway. Uh-oh. What he probably saw through the driving snow was me angrily shaking my fist at him. I'd have to repair the damage later. I headed inside with my bounty. Zach, observing the snow in my eyebrows and hair, seeing me clutching my prized herbs in frozen fingers, just shook his head.

I felt I owed him some kind of explanation, in his own vernacular. "Dried thyme sucks," I said, and proceeded to the kitchen to prepare my gratin.

Venturing into a snowstorm to pick herbs may seem like slightly eccentric behavior from the old man, I'll admit. But one reason why I have the kitchen garden is that it *allows* me to cook with fresh herbs in February. I think. Maybe it's the other way around. Perhaps I seek out recipes requiring fresh thyme in February because I know I happen to have it and want to use it. Put more succinctly, do I cook because I garden, or garden because I cook?

One thing is certain: having the garden does change the *way* I cook, as I am always looking for innovative things to do with the harvest. Without the garden, would I ever have discovered the simple delight of Russian banana fingerling potatoes roasted with olive oil, kosher salt, and fresh rosemary? Doubt it. Nor would I have experimented with pairing pasta and sage, something I tried on a whim only because I had three varieties of sage growing and needed something to do with it. Likewise, in late August, I am constantly fiddling around with tomatoes, looking for new things to do with them, slow-roasting them in the oven, chopping them into different salsas in combination with other fresh crops (our family favorite: tomato-peach-mint salsa), making fresh and cooked pasta sauces, and constructing unstable towers with mozzarella and basil. And certainly, without the garden, Katie and I would never, ever have made windowpane pasta with nasturtium butter.

This memorable project started innocently enough, when I placed a new cookbook, one of those large-format ones with a color photograph of every recipe, in front of Katie one summer morning. "What should we make for lunch Saturday? Do you want to see if anything here looks interesting?"

Jack and his wife, Pam, were coming over, and I didn't have a menu yet. I knew we were going to start with broiled Brandywine tomatoes, each thick slice topped with a basil leaf, olive oil, and freshly grated Pecorino Romano, but I was stumped on the main course.

"How about this?" Katie said a few minutes later, pointing

to a photograph of pasta squares somehow imprinted with real herb leaves, covered in a rich butter sauce and garnished with edible nasturtium and violet flowers.

I gulped hard. Asking me to make fresh pasta for Jack and Pam was like handing a shell-shocked soldier a rifle and sending him back to the front. It had been nearly twenty years since I had dared make fresh pasta for company. That first and last experience had been so traumatic I'd retired the pasta machine. If that wasn't enough, the guests that night had been none other than Jack and Pam!

Anxious to use my new Italian pasta machine, and anxious to impress not only my friends but my new girlfriend, Anne, I had decided to make carrot fettuccine in a cream sauce. The pasta dough, which I made in the food processor, took on a lovely pale orange hue from the pureed carrots, and all was going well until I tried to send the pasta through the machine.

A pasta machine is simply a pair of adjustable rollers and a crank. Starting at the widest roller setting, and narrowing the space between the rollers with each pass, you feed the dough into the rollers with one hand while turning the crank with the other hand, receiving the rolled pasta with the—um—other hand.

Precisely. That's *three* hands. I had only two. If I used my left hand to feed, and let the too-sticky dough pile up on the outfeed side, the pasta ribbon folded back onto itself in a glutinous mess. If I moved my left hand to receive the rolled pasta, the dough I was feeding stuck to the top of the machine and tore. As I repeated sending the pasta through the machine, the dough becoming thinner and more delicate with each pass, this problem became more and more acute. Eventually I somehow managed to roll it all out, resorting to a rolling pin at times, and then cut it into strips of fettuccine.

The fettuccine needed to be dried. I have since read that fresh pasta can be dried perfectly well laid flat on a floured surface or dish towel, but the cookbook I was using advised suspending the pasta from a drying rack. Thus the previous day I had built a rack based on one I had seen in a catalog, consisting of dowels set into a pine board. A couple of hooks at the top allowed me to mount the rack on a door so that the long strips of pasta draped over the dowels would have room to hang.

I laid the last of my carrot fettuccine strips over the dowels as my guests were arriving. They were, I have to say, quite impressed at the sight of these two-foot-long pale orange pasta strips, decorating my door like Christmas tree tinsel. It was a proud moment. Anne smiled, I thought even lovingly. We all sat in the small kitchen as I poured some wine.

Plop. What was that? A strip of pasta had landed on the kitchen floor. Our heads turned as one to the rack. Before our eyes, *plop*, a second strip simply broke in half and dropped to the floor. I raced to the rack as other strips started falling. As the pasta dried and became brittle, it was snapping under its own weight. Jack and Pam were hysterical. Anne jumped to my side, trying to be the supportive girlfriend, but was having a hard time seeing through her tears of laughter.

The rest of the evening is but a blur. Somehow I salvaged the fettuccine, but I have never lived down the dinner. And now, Katie was offering a return to the nightmare. Or redemption.

I told her my story.

"Then you *have* to make this," she insisted.

I looked at the book. "I don't know, Katie. This isn't a recipe; this is a science project."

"I'll help!" she pleaded. "I'll be your third hand."

Now, how could I resist an offer like that? Besides, it was a spectacular-looking dish, something I was sure our guests had never had (and would never have again), and I liked the way it featured the garden, since we had a nice array of herbs available, as well as plenty of nasturtiums and violets. What the heck.

Saturday morning, Katie shook me out of bed, and we went into the garden to pick herbs and tomatoes. With steady hands I pulled the pasta machine from the shelf, blew off the dust, and we proceeded to make pasta. I fed and cranked while Katie, standing on a chair, received the dough, and then we cut the pasta into three-inch-wide strips. Katie artfully arranged patterns of sage, parsley, basil, and dill on half of the strips. Then we laid an unadorned strip atop each of the herbed ones and fed the resulting sandwich through the machine several times until the pasta was thin enough to become translucent, the herbs — pressed out like leaves under glass — easily visible inside. We dried the strips on the floured countertop without incident and cut the pasta into squares. By the time we were done, Katie knew the names of all the herbs in the garden, and my love for making pasta had been restored.

Jack and Pam laughed and shared a nostalgic moment when they heard we were serving homemade pasta, but the laughter stopped when Katie brought out the dish. It was visually stunning, the herbs from our garden glowing inside the little windows of pasta, which were glazed with a glistening butter sauce and adorned with orange nasturtiums and blue violets. The windowpane pasta with nasturtium butter, I have to admit, looked better than it tasted, but I'll bet that no one remembers that today. Certainly, as a culinary tour de force to impress your friends and chase away an old ghost, it was hard to top. Best of all, Katie and I now make fresh pasta several times a year.

THE STORY THAT MARCO POLO introduced pasta to Italy upon his return from China has been debunked, which is too bad, because were it true, it would make spaghetti and tomato sauce, that quintessential Italian dish, a fusion of Oriental and Aztec cuisine! For it is fairly certain that tomatoes originated in South America and were introduced from Central America to Europe shortly after the Spanish conquistador Cortés defeated the

Aztec city of Tenochtitlán (today Mexico City) in 1521. Yet it was the Italians, not the Spaniards, who fully embraced and saw the culinary possibilities of this strange fruited vine the Aztecs called *xitomatl*.

What were these Aztec tomatoes like? Certainly they were no beefsteak or Early Girl, but we would readily recognize these small, tough-skinned orbs as tomatoes today. But probably not red tomatoes. The earliest-known citation of the tomato in literature, in 1544 by the sixteenth-century writer and herbalist Petrus Matthiolus, refers to Italians eating *pomi d'oro,* or "golden apples," suggesting that the first tomatoes introduced to Europe were more yellow than red. The name stuck even after red tomatoes were introduced, again probably by Spanish conquistadors or missionaries; thus the contemporary Italian word for tomato is *pomodoro.* Matthiolus, by the way, writes that Italians simply ate them with olive oil, salt, and pepper, which sounds strikingly modern, as though the dish were lifted off the summer lunch menu at Union Square Café.

The tomato flourished in Italy's mild Mediterranean climate. It would still be a while before tomatoes found spaghetti—the first-known published recipe for a pasta-and-tomato dish doesn't appear until 1839—but the tomatoes were at least in the kitchen. The same could not be said for northern Europe, where *xitomatl* was catching on a little more slowly. The English in particular, who grew tomatoes as ornamentals (nonedible plants), were initially convinced that the fruits were poisonous, possibly because of the plant's uncanny resemblance to a relative named—for good reason—deadly nightshade, *Atropa belladonna.* Other northern European peoples were wary as well. In fact, in the eighteenth century the great Swedish taxonomist Carolus Linnaeus bestowed upon the tomato the botanical name *Lycopersicon esculentum,* literally "edible wolf peach," perhaps an indication of its public image. So while northern Europeans were avoiding tomatoes like, well, the plague, Italians were busy breeding cultivars and inventing lasagna.

This would not be the first time that Europeans would view a New World plant with suspicion. Potatoes, also South American natives, met a similarly cool reception when introduced shortly after tomatoes. As late as 1744, Prussian peasants refused to eat this starchy vegetable that Frederick the Great had sent to relieve their famine—until forced to at the end of a bayonet.

That both the tomato and the potato originated somewhere around Peru should not be too surprising: they are botanical relatives, both being in the Solanaceae family. Personally, I had always viewed this alleged botanical relationship with some skepticism—after all, they seem to have absolutely nothing in common—until I grew both potatoes and Brandywine tomatoes in my garden, and the similarities revealed themselves. For unlike the classic, sharply lobed leaf seen in most tomato varieties, the

Brandywine heirloom has flat leaves that look remarkably like potato foliage. In fact, they are so distinctive that I don't bother to label the plants when I start them on the windowsill or set them in the garden; there is no mistaking them for other tomatoes.

As further evidence of their familial relationship, potato flowers bear a fair resemblance to tomato flowers and even develop tiny green fruits that look like baby tomatoes. Sometimes it takes a home garden to make a believer of a skeptic.

Tomatoes may first have been cultivated after they traveled to Central America (practically down the block, geographically speaking), but the tomatoes in my home garden and yours derive from European, not Central American, cultivars. The tomato completed its curious round-trip back to the New World in the baggage of European settlers. As the first colonists were primarily northern European, not southern Italian, the tomato was not originally grown in the colonies as a food but was instead treated as an ornamental or, at best, a plant with some medicinal properties. Still, the fact that the colonists took the trouble to include tomato seeds in their transatlantic luggage suggests that they thought fairly highly of them.

It wasn't until the early nineteenth century that the tomato, a full three hundred years after Cortés, made its way into American kitchens, though. In fact, among the first American gardeners (not counting the Aztecs, of course) to grow tomatoes for food was none other than my old hero: statesman, orchardist, visionary, and *tomato farmer* Thomas Jefferson! This third president of the United States served tomatoes at a White House dinner in 1806 and grew them annually after retiring to Monticello in 1809. This was at a time when most Americans still viewed tomatoes with suspicion, many believing they were poisonous.

Incidentally, potatoes started to become popular in America at about the same time as tomatoes, and guess who is credited with introducing french fries (not to mention the first pasta machine) to America. Yes, him again.

HUNDREDS OF YEARS AGO, Italians discovered that tomatoes could be preserved through the winter by drying them on their tile roofs. Thus the sun-dried tomato was born, though it was most likely considered a distant second-best to fresh tomatoes, not the gourmet item that today adds a dollar to the price of your salad. Anne and I had dreamed about making our own sun-dried tomatoes the night we lay under that starry sky awaiting Big Machinery, and indeed the following year we set up production. And it *was* a production.

Not having a tile roof, I made a large wooden frame in the shop (why is it that so many of my culinary projects begin in the woodshop?) and stapled to it a galvanized screen. This took the entire morning, as it necessitated one trip to the lumberyard and two trips to the hardware store (I ran out of staples). Then we harvested dozens of cherry tomatoes, sliced each in half, and placed them on the screen. We put the frame in the sun and waited for the tomatoes to dehydrate.

The reason that sun-dried tomatoes are so tasty lies in the chemistry of the fruit. Tomatoes contain significant amounts of both sugar and acid, part of the appeal of dried and fresh tomatoes alike. But never is the sugar/acid balance more apparent than in dried tomatoes, for after the moisture and most of the weight has evaporated, the intense essence of the tomato is unmasked, and each bite is both tangy and sweet, tart and toothsome. A lot of taste in a very small package. There may be another reason why tomatoes—especially these concentrated, sun-dried tomatoes—are so tasty, and so adept at flavoring other foods: they are high in glutamic acid, the naturally occurring form of the flavor enhancer MSG (monosodium glutamate). This might explain why we love to dip our french fries in ketchup and why a mere dollop of tomato paste makes a beef stew so much tastier. Even the British, when they were still shunning fresh tomatoes, had started using them sparingly to improve their soups.

Food chemistry aside, Anne and I were greatly looking forward to a winter of sun-dried tomatoes. After days of lugging them inside at night on the rack to keep off the dew (it took two of us to carry the frame) and moving them back outside in the morning, we still didn't think they seemed quite dry. But who knew how dry is dry? Well, *now* I know: dry is drier than you can get tomatoes in New York in August, when for days at a time, the humidity might never drop below 80 percent. When a rain front moved in and stayed, we decided these tomatoes were as dry as they were going to get, so we brought them inside and bottled them. Within a couple of months, they were boasting the most lovely white mold. They were obviously inedible, although I thought, given the love and attention we had lavished on these tomatoes, the mold might hold some miraculous medicinal property, a new penicillin.

I'll never know, because we dumped them into the garbage rather than turn them over to science. We never tried to sun-dry tomatoes again. Instead we get a similar effect by making what some call tomato confit, slow-roasting quartered, seasoned tomatoes in a slow oven for a couple of hours.

As with many of my failures, I did salvage something good out of it. I found another use for the drying frame: screening compost. Every time I pull it out, I remember that furry, luxuriant white mold. And wonder if I threw away the cure for cancer.

JUST WHAT IS THIS PLANT that spawned the fuzzy mold—a fruit or a vegetable? This somewhat tired debate would probably have been dismissed with a gloved

wave from Jefferson two hundred years ago. Yet it was re-
newed recently when several New Jersey state legislators
introduced a bill naming the tomato the official state
vegetable, sparking a weird partisan debate in the state-
house — Democrats claimed it was a vegetable, Republicans insisted it was a fruit. I have a hard enough time
as it is explaining to Katie the ideological differences
between Republicans and Democrats. How to explain
this one?

When more than a few observers pointed out with some
glee that the tomato is indeed a fruit, embarrassed leg-
islative aides went scurrying and dug up a century-old
U.S. Supreme Court ruling that declared the tomato to be
a vegetable, at least for the purposes of the Tariff Act of
1883. Democratic legislators proudly waved this narrow
ruling about import duties in front of the television cam-
eras but had to be careful about which sections they
quoted from, because the Court, in its decision, flatly
stated, "Botanically speaking, tomatoes are fruits of a
vine." In fact, the tomato is not only botanically a fruit (because it is a ripened mature ovary containing seeds, and
that happens to be the very definition of a fruit), it is
specifically a berry, which is something to consider the
next time you pop a cherry tomato into your mouth.

Thus there really isn't much to debate here. We may not
have heard the end of this story, though. Almost hilari-
ously, this campaign to name the tomato the official state

vegetable happened a mere year after a losing attempt (to the blueberry) to name the tomato the official state *fruit*! I fear that if the tomato loses out again, next year some determined legislator will try to get it designated the state animal. Jefferson must be rolling in his grave.

Christopher Walken, Gardener

You got the wrong guy, Ace.
—Christopher Walken in *The Deer Hunter*

A ugust. Heavy-hot, sticky-still August. The garden was five years old. I was approaching fifty. The air was thick with the heavy, pungent smell of fresh horse manure, steaming faintly from its towering heap. Anne and I had brought it in over the weekend, in 18-gallon Rubbermaid bins, from a nearby stable. We made four trips—sixteen bins, 288 gallons of horseshit—shoveling wordlessly side by side as we filled and loaded, filled and loaded. We had made arrangements through a mutual friend of the owner's, and when we drove up, the owner at first ignored us. When we finally got her attention, she apologized, saying, "I figured you couldn't be the folks comin' for the manure. Not in a Saab." And I thought, *She's right.* How absurd we must have looked, the doctor and her husband shoveling manure into their

Saab station wagon. There was probably a dichotomy there worth exploring, but not on this day. Too tired. Too hot.

It looked as though the groundhog had found a way in and had once again taken a single bite from half a dozen tomatoes. Does he have to do that? I would gladly grant him six bites of one tomato; why does he have to ruin six tomatoes by taking a single bite out of each? Is he finicky? Is he always disappointed with that first bite and hopes the next tomato will be sweeter? Groundhogs do seem pretty selective when it comes to choosing tomatoes. I have never, I mean never, seen a groundhog eat an unripe tomato. They always seem to eat the tomato one day before you plan to pick it. Do they judge by color or by smell? If color, could I trick them by growing only varieties of tomato that are green when ripe? Although that doesn't sound very appetizing to me, either. Anyway, I think they judge ripeness by smell. I vaguely remember reading somewhere that groundhogs, like most burrowers, have very poor vision.

I flung the bitten tomatoes into the tall grass in the failed meadow and walked down the unmowed center grass path to the vine bed as the August morning sun drew beads of sweat from my temple. The vine bed was a depressing sight, unkempt and thick with weeds and clumps of bluegrass, littered with the last unpicked, rotting cucumbers, bloated and yellowish. For that matter, *I* was a depressing sight, unshowered, unshaven, and bloated from a steady summer diet of BLTs, feeling exhausted, slovenly, and lazy. I wondered, *Am I becoming my garden, or is my garden becoming me?*

After five years of toiling, I had begun to question the entire enterprise. My early-morning drives to the garden center for yet more mulch or to the stable for yet more horse manure took me past a golf club, where on any given day, dozens of men my age were passing their mornings socializing and (mildly) exercising and apparently having one hell of a good time. Why had I locked myself in a self-imposed purgatory of endless weeding, pruning, and harvesting? This was what I did for fun?

I flopped down on a bench to think about this. I know there was certainly one reason I persisted: we were hooked on the food. On vine-ripened Brandywine tomatoes, on crisp sugar snap peas, earthy-tasting potatoes, and greens that awaken your mouth. In other words, I was farming.

At some point, without even realizing it, I had crossed a line. I remembered a stupendous dinner we had one Autumn evening: pork roast with apples, acorn squash, baby lettuces, Peruvian potatoes. Anne pointed out with pride that everything except the pork came from our garden, and I stopped in midbite, intrigued. Pig farming. Could we, I wondered out loud, raise a couple of pigs? Just think, fresh, organic pork. Forks froze in midair. Mouths stopped chewing. Silence smothered the table as three terrified faces stared at me, then at one another, not sure if I was kidding. I wasn't sure if I was kidding.

But on this oppressive August morning, I was sure of this: my interest in gardening as hobby was waning, as was the purely aesthetic appeal the garden once held for me. I had to figure this out, and soon. I (more than anyone, probably) didn't want to give up the food, either, but the growing of it was wrecking me. I had to reduce the labor. And the first place to start with was with the grass, the goddamn grass.

Those lovely paths that our landscape architect had seduced me into were killing me. On the day Bridget proudly unrolled the garden plan, with its broad strip of grass down the center and narrower strips along each side, I intuitively felt it was a bad idea, but as it turned out, not for all the right reasons. She insisted it would look "grand," and Anne and I deferred to her professional judgment and succumbed to her gorgeous smile. And indeed, it *was* grand—I have to give her credit for that. After all, it was only a few strips of grass; how hard could it be to mow? Since we had Carmine and crew to mow the rest of the yard with his forty-eight-inch mowers, I could surely spend a few minutes each week mowing the garden. It did seem very—well, English, I guess. Still, I'd had vague misgivings.

That first summer, the grass came in like wildfire, Kentucky bluegrass wildfire. In no time at all, a thick, lush carpet of green neatly bisected and enclosed the beds, and it was time to mow. But to bring a noisy, fume-spewing gasoline engine into the garden seemed a sacrilege. In an English-gentleman moment of delusion, I decided I would purchase a hand mower to use in the garden and the orchard. I had been eyeing the $400 model in the Smith & Hawken catalog for some time. "This is not your father's mower," the copy promised. Indeed not. This was a silent, finely tuned instrument, crafted in Germany, land of Henckels kitchen cutlery and the Mercedes-Benz, where they still know a thing or two about blades and craftsmanship. Why, I'd want to cut the lawn every day with an instrument like this. But $400! There was another model I'd seen, the L.L. Bean Classic Reel Mower, "quiet, safe, and reliable" with a "scissor-like tip." And only $139. I wanted to buy it, but Anne suggested that I first look at Home Depot.

"Home Depot!" I sniffed. "I wouldn't buy a mower from there. They just carry junk. L.L. Bean has scoured the globe to find just the right mower for their catalog [and for their not-quite-affluent, snobbish clientele like me] and I think I trust them a little more."

Nevertheless, I stopped in at Home Depot just to humor my wife. They had the exact same mower as in the L.L. Bean catalog, for $79. I might be a snob, but I'm not stupid. I brought it home. In retrospect I like to think I bought this mower so *you* don't have to, so let me try to explain why the gasoline-powered rotary mower is far and away the most popular mower in the world.

The Classic Reel Mower does not cut tall grass. It does fine in grass that is one or two inches higher than the height you are cutting it to (grass that, in my book, doesn't really need to be cut yet). Anything more than that, and the grass hits what the industry calls the shrub bar, a steel bar that protrudes across the front of the mower. The purpose of the bar is presumably to deflect shrubbery so that you don't accidentally mow down your shrubs. In practice it deflects tall grass as well, so you can't cut tall grass, either. And in the spring (and this was spring), the grass is *always* tall. Ten minutes after you cut it, it's ready for a trim.

The Classic Reel Mower cannot mow backward. This should be patently obvious, even to an idiot like me, when you stop to think about it, since the blades are set spinning from the forward motion of the wheels. But after years of using a power rotary mower, you unwittingly develop the habit of going back and forth, especially under trees and around tight spots. The kind of trees and tight spots you might find in, say, an orchard or a garden. Additionally, when pulled backward, the mower tends to lift up rather than roll back, so you end up literally carrying the mower around the yard.

The Classic Reel Mower cannot trim close to walls, fences, or other objects. On a rotary mower, the wheels are set at about two, four, eight, and ten o'clock, so you can get the housing pretty close to an adjoining wall at three or nine o'clock. But a reel mower is linear in shape, with a pair of big, clunky wheels on either end, so you cannot get closer than five or six inches to a wall. Since most of my grass paths bordered either a stone wall or raised beds, I was unable to cut almost a quarter of the grass.

All I can say is, thank goodness I found all this out with a $79 mower, not a $400 one, which shares all these inherent problems. In the end I wound up cutting the grass with my old Sears rotary, but that was no picnic, either. Each path was about two and a half mower widths wide, and maneuvering the mower to make a U-turn while keeping my feet out of the beds at the end of each narrow path required ballerina-like agility. And even with a rotary mower, I never could cut the grass that grew along the jagged stone retaining walls, so every couple of weeks, I had to come in with that nastiest of power tools, the Weedwacker.

This was sheer torture for me, as using the Weedwacker requires first putting on long pants and finding safety goggles and ear plugs, then yanking on the starter rope and fiddling with the choke for five minutes until it comes roaring to life. Then you pray that the "bump" mechanism, which feeds the orange plastic cord, continues to work; otherwise you have to take the device to the workshop, disassemble it, and rewind the cord (and repeat two or three times) until it finally works. And where, I'd like to know, does all that plastic cord go? I ran through a twenty-five-foot roll in a season, so somewhere there must be twenty-five feet of pulverized plastic cord incorporated into my garden beds. Not a pleasant thought.

Thus I was not happy about the grass paths I had been talked into, but the worst was yet to come. Bridget and George had used, of all things, Kentucky bluegrass. Homeowners love lawns of bluegrass. Why? For the same reason that bluegrass does not belong in a meadow. *It spreads like a weed.* Not all grasses share this behavior. Perennial rye, which I used in the meadow, does not. Neither does tall fescue. But bluegrass does, which makes it particularly unsuited to a garden, a fact that became painfully obvious as it rapidly made its way into the beds. Seemingly overnight, weeds—actual weeds—had become an afterthought, as my weeding sessions were dominated by pulling out clumps of bluegrass. If I wasn't vigilant, the border between grass and bed became indistinguishable. Clumps of grass sprouted from the stone retaining walls like air ferns.

I was not enjoying myself. I wanted to spend my time in the garden gardening, not tending to runaway grass, and the frustration was mounting rapidly. So on this August day, I suggested to Anne that we get rid of all the grass and put in gravel paths.

"But it's so—*grand,*" she protested, obviously still brainwashed, smitten, or both. "Is there something else we could do that would make it easier to deal with?"

I thought for a while, and eventually it seemed that

installing steel edging along the paths might help. The edging would give us a clean division between lawn and bed and, with any luck, cut down on the invasive spread of the bluegrass's underground runners. And we could fill the space between the edging and the stone terraces with mulch and thyme, allowing us to drop two wheels of the lawn mower inside the edging and cut all the grass cleanly, eliminating the need for weed whacking.

It seemed like the way to go. There was only one problem: I dreaded the thought of doing yet more labor. Make no mistake, this was backbreaking work, digging a small trench with a spade and laying in the edging. To hire someone would cost a fortune. So I procrastinated. And complained about the grass. And procrastinated. Until finally Anne had had enough, and one Sunday afternoon she announced, "I'm buying you a gardener." This was to be my Christmas present. Okay, it beats a necktie, but I was skeptical.

"You'll never find someone to do a small job like this," I predicted.

Anne slid the local newspaper across the table. "What about him?"

I looked at the classifieds. "Experienced gardener available for weeding, gardening, cleanup. No job too big or too small." A local phone number. He was in town. And he didn't have a hyphenated company name. I avoid contractors with hyphenated names, as in Jay-Dan. These are

invariably two-man operations formed by a couple of bud-
dies who got the brilliant idea to draw up a partnership on
a cocktail napkin over one too many beers at the bar, who
are inevitably going to end up fighting over money or a
woman or both, becoming ex-buddies in the process and
dissolving the business. Any day now. Besides, if Jay and
Dan can't come up with a more imaginative name than
Jay-Dan (or Dan-Jay), they don't deserve my business.

So this prospect did seem promising. "Okay, give him
a call."

Now, as any homeowner knows, calling represents
merely the first step of the lengthy process of getting a contractor to your house for an estimate. Any painter, plumber,
electrician, or gardener worth his salt does not come right
over to the house. In fact he doesn't answer his phone. You
leave a message on his answering machine, and he calls
back in the middle of a weekday when he knows you
couldn't possibly be home and leaves a message on *your*
machine. And even if you just missed his call, even if you
walked into the house as he was hanging up, if you call the
number he leaves you on the machine thirty seconds later,
he will not answer. You will get *his* machine. And so on.
Until, when the planets finally align in the house of Jupiter
and you establish voice contact, he makes an appointment
for a week from Tuesday. And shows up an hour late. If he's
really good, he stands you up entirely and you have to return to step one to reschedule.

The better the contractor, the more difficult he is to get ahold of. So I was rather startled—and a little concerned—when Anne hung up the phone and said, "He's coming right over." Now? On a Sunday afternoon? What seemed like only moments later, a movement caught my eye. I turned around and looked out the window, and Christopher Walken was standing in my garden.

He was, I would guess, in his early thirties, with close-cropped hair, sunken cheeks, and the eerie gray eyes of an assassin. He bore a remarkable resemblance, not only physically, it would turn out, but in mannerism as well, to the actor Christopher Walken. So much so that to this day neither Anne nor I can remember his real name, first or last. We still refer to him as Christopher Walken. I gathered my composure and went out to meet him.

I AM ALWAYS A LITTLE uncomfortable when introducing myself to contractors, despite the practice that an old home affords. My problem is, I am never quite sure which persona to present to a tradesman. On the one hand, I may have learned some blue-collar skills over the years, but there is no denying (or hiding) my white-collar pedigree. When the white-collar side of me prevails, I feel I risk alienation (and a higher estimate). I've heard contractors complaining about the "rich, dumb bastards" they work for, and since I am neither rich nor dumb, and hope I'm not a bastard, I'd rather not be lumped in with that group. On the other hand, I have over the years acquired

a fair range of skills in carpentry, plumbing, woodworking, and even electricity, so I can meet a tradesman in my
jeans and speak pretty knowledgeably about the job he
is being engaged for. Sometimes too knowledgeably, for
this has often backfired. I can't count how many times a
contractor has said to me something like, "You seem
handy — what if I just frame it out, and you can put up the
Sheetrock." (Note the lack of a question mark at the end
of that sentence.) And because contractors and I both hate
the same things, they get to do the "fun" stuff, and I'm left
hanging Sheetrock and cursing through my breath. It has
gotten to the point that I literally hide in the bedroom
when someone comes over to give an estimate, so Anne
can play the helpless housewife and make sure the whole
job gets done without my having to finish it up. This
sometimes creates quite a comical scene.

"Quick, he's here. Hide!" Anne calls as I fly up the
stairs like an illicit boyfriend hiding from the husband
who's arrived home unexpectedly.

The other issue we have to deal with — and I don't expect much sympathy on this count — is Anne's profession.
Some contractors charge what the market, that is the
client, will bear. During the initial meeting, these contractors will size up your finances and factor that into the bid.
While you think you're making small talk, the contractor
is studying you, your house, and your property and trying
to figure out how affluent you are and how high he can go
with his bid. When we first bought our house, this worked

in our favor, as it was a ninety-year-old wreck. But I have seen how influential the contractor's perception of your wealth can be. I vividly remember one case when we had some carpentry done for a very reasonable figure (although naturally I had to do the trim work myself). We paid by check and, less than a year later, called the carpenter in to do another job. He greeted us warmly, "Hi, Bill. Hi, Doctor." *Doctor?* Last summer she was "Anne." The estimate came in at almost double what we had expected.

"Why did his prices go up so much?" Anne asked.

"Gee, I can't imagine, *Doctor*," I answered.

"Doctor inflation?" she said, coining a new term, her eyes wide. "You know, I wouldn't mind if I actually made a doctor's salary."

As a primary-care physician practicing old-fashioned medicine in the modern world, she doesn't make Marcus Welby's income. I sometimes ask her when she's going to stop "practicing" and go into business.

"How did he know I'm a doctor?" Anne wondered. She was still working out of town at the time.

I placed the checkbook down in front of her, jabbing my finger on the "MD" after her name. Ironically, Anne had never wanted it included on the checks (she only uses her title professionally); it was I who insisted on it after she graduated from medical school, convincing her she had worked hard for those two little initials and ought to use them. Now I was sorry I had. After a similar experience with doctor inflation, we discussed removing the "MD," but since we figured that we were done with contractors for a while, we left it on. What we didn't yet realize was that when you own a ninety-year-old house, you are never, ever done with contractors. Today, with Anne having her own practice in town and counting among her patients some of our contractors, there are no secrets left, so the costly initials remain for good.

THE INTERVIEW WITH Christopher Walken, which I couldn't hide from, got off to a bad start.

"Beautiful place. How much property?"

Some people would be flattered by this question. I always feel a little embarrassed, as if the next question might be, "How much did you pay for it?"

I told him three acres. He nodded. "How much did you pay for it?"

I was a little taken aback. "Uh, not that much. Foreclosure."

To move him off the subject, I started to explain the edging project, but he seemed more interested in the large, slightly bloody bandage on my left hand.

"So you understand what I want here?" I asked.

"What happened to your hand?" he replied.

I had recently sliced off the tip of my left index finger on the table saw. In the emergency room, the nurse tending me had asked me where I lived. I decided to skip the preliminaries.

"The Big Brown House," I said.

She knew exactly what I meant.

"I used to live there. I kept a horse in the barn."

So that explains all the hay I'd had to lug out when building the woodshop.

"Is it still a barn?"

"More like a slaughterhouse," I said ruefully, holding up my finger.

The surgeon expertly sewed my finger back together, but I'll never play the violin.

I told Christopher Walken I'd had a slight accident in the shop, sparing him (to his chagrin, I'm sure) the painful details, and finally got him focused on the edging. Christopher had lots of questions and advice, delivered with a gravity worthy of a neurosurgeon discussing your imminent brain surgery. All the while I couldn't get over the resemblance to that famous actor; it was downright spooky. As was the gardener. But he did seem to know what he was talking about. It turned out he was fairly new to town and was living as a kind of handyman-gardener-caretaker on an elderly woman's property—"the estate," he called it, as if no other identification were required. He had an uncanny way of working the phrase "on the estate" into every other sentence, as in "The way we do this on the estate . . ." or "Have you seen how I trimmed back those lilacs on the estate?" Anne and I had no idea what he was talking about, and no idea of where in our tiny village anything resembling an "estate" could possibly be located.

As so often happens with contractors, instead of my interviewing him, he ended up interviewing me. And as I said, he had lots of questions. Some of them good questions, about how high I wanted the edging, and others about how much work we had to keep him employed beyond the edging job. The truth was, I had accumulated enough undone tasks to keep him busy through the fall. I could get used to having a personal gardener. In the end we agreed on initially committing to hiring him (or maybe he hired us) to do the edging and two clearing jobs. He was ready to start the edging Monday morning. As in, *tomorrow*. Okay, so he wasn't in great demand right now. He'd just moved to town, so maybe it was no reflection on his skills. Still, I wondered . . .

Because the edging came in ten-foot sections, and he had a pickup truck and I didn't, we agreed that I would stop by the Agway store early Monday morning and pay for the materials, and he would pick them up shortly after.

When I got home from work Monday evening, I was impressed with how much work had been done. I was standing in the garden admiring it in the setting sun when a voice from behind startled me.

"Everything all right?" he said. I almost jumped out of my skin. How *did* he materialize out of nowhere?

"Oh, Chris—" I caught myself just in time. "It looks great. You got a lot done today."

He leveled his assassin's eyes at me. "It's hard work. Really hard." A pause.

I didn't know what he was driving at or quite how to respond. "If it was easy, I'd be doing it myself" didn't seem appropriate. I mumbled something like, "I know. I've done my share of digging. But it looks great. Thanks so much."

He waited, I guess, for more, until he decided I had missed my cue, then continued, "I was just wondering if you could pay me for today. Cash."

Oh. I hadn't realized that was our financial arrangement. I went into the kitchen and raided the grocery money and borrowed forty dollars from Zach.

By the next evening, the job was almost done. On cue, Christopher Walken materialized, looking even more tightly wound than usual, if that was possible. He had some bad, really bad, news. "They shorted you half the spikes."

The spikes were narrow triangular pieces of metal that got pounded into loops on the edging and served both to attach the edging to the ground and to secure adjoining sections together. They were utterly critical to the installation.

"Are you sure?"

His colorless eyes narrowed and his mainspring tightened another click. He looked as if he wanted to slit my throat. "Do you think I'm *lying* to you?" he asked, dragging out the word as if the very notion was incomprehensible.

"No, no, of course not. It's just surprising that they would do that. They're pretty good over there," I explained. "And I suspect they're going to give me a hard time over it."

"They're a bunch of assholes. And if they give you any problem, I'll come over there and—"

"Let's just see what happens." I had a *Deer Hunter* flashback and shivered. "Okay, exactly how many short are we?"

We counted the remaining sections and spikes, finding a couple that Christopher had mislaid in the grass. We were exactly a full bundle—that is, ten—short.

The next morning, I left for work a half-hour early and swung by Agway. If there is anything I hate doing, it's showing up at the farm store or the lumberyard in a tie. It marks you as a tenderfoot. A softy. Definitely not one of the boys. And when you're going in with a dispute, you really, really want to be one of the boys.

But there I was in my tie and pressed shirt. I told them about the missing spikes. They were polite but skeptical. The woman out front called in the yardman who had handled the order.

"I remember counting them out myself," he said softly but firmly. "They must still be in his truck. That truck was some mess."

"He swears they're not. Is it possible he left them behind?"

"Well, they would still be here if he did. I'll go take another look."

He came back a few minutes later. No such luck. I pleaded, "Look, if you can give me replacements, I'll pay you for them."

"If I had extras, I'd give them to you for nothing. But they only give us enough spikes for the sections of edging they ship. If I give these to you, I can't sell the remaining edging."

I was not about to buy a half-dozen more sections, at thirty dollars apiece, just to get the spikes. I didn't know what to do, and I told them so. I must have looked as if I was going to cry. The yardman went out back and returned with a handful of spikes. He extended them to me. "You can leave out some of the center ones. This should get you through the job." I thanked him profusely. "By the way, who is your gardener?" he asked. "I've never seen him before. He's a little . . . strange."

"Christopher Walken," I said over my shoulder as I walked out of the store. "Didn't you recognize him?"

Now thoroughly late for work, I raced home with my precious bounty. Walken was unloading his truck. I started to relate my trip to Agway, which I immediately realized was a mistake. His eyes flashed with anger—the first sign of life I had ever seen in them—his face reddened, his neck swelled, and he started to stride toward his truck.

"Where are you going?" I cried after him.

"Why, I'm going to go punch him right in the nose."

Now, I know this sounds like bad movie dialogue from

the thirties, but that is exactly what he said: "Why, I'm going to go punch him right in the nose."

I quickly put myself between him and the truck. "You don't want to do that."

"No one calls me a liar!"

"No one is calling you a liar, Chr—" Whoops. "He just thinks he gave you the right amount. Maybe we should look in your truck once more."

His eyes flashed again. "Are *you* calling me a liar?"

No, I was thinking. *Just a psychopath.* I tried to be diplomatic. "Look, it doesn't really matter who's at fault. He gave me some extra spikes; let's see if we can make do with what we have."

Christopher sulked for a while. I drove to the office, trying to push the image of Christopher Walken laying waste to the Agway out of my head. On the radio an old Talking Heads song was playing, and I sang along with a new lyric: "Psycho gardener, better run, run a-waaaaaay."

Christopher Walken managed to finish the job and stayed with us for another week, clearing two weedy, shrubby areas where we wanted to plant grass or ground cover. Each evening, he showed up to collect his day's wages and to complain about how hard the work was. After several days he felt comfortable enough with me to start sharing some intimacies about his difficult life.

We've gotten to know some of our contractors rather well. Several, as I've mentioned, are Anne's patients. More than a few of the tradesmen in this town are natives whose family trades go back a generation or more, a tradition more commonly found in a European village than in modern America. My plumber, for example, now eighty, is in business with his son. Before that, he was in business with his *father*. These second- and third-generation tradesmen tend to be the most reliable because of their long-term view of the business.

They are also the friendliest and most enjoyable to have around and are more likely to be in no rush to either come or go. Whenever plumber père comes to the house, I make sure I have a pot of coffee ready. This guarantees me a half hour of captivating tales of plumber *grand-père* working on my house and the surrounding estate (now, *that* was an estate) during the Great Depression.

I was not ready to sit down to coffee—which I could easily see escalating to Russian roulette in a Vietnamese gambling den—with Christopher Walken. But the details and the sadness of his life dripped out a little day by day. He was a single father with a teenage son, just trying to get by, to be a good father. He'd had a lot of "bad breaks," he seemed to want me to know. I wanted to be sympathetic, but there was always an undercurrent of comparing what he saw as my "privileged" life to his, and it made me feel uncomfortable. On some level, maybe his campaign—if that's what it was—was working, because despite his spookiness, by the end of the week, when he was finished with the clearing jobs, Anne and I, knowing all too well that good gardeners are next to impossible to find, were considering keeping him on for a few more jobs, maybe even permanently.

That is, until I planted the grass on the newly cleared ground. This was to be an easy job. Christopher Walken had done (as he reminded me daily) all the hard work. All I had to do was lightly rake it over, scatter some seed, and throw on some straw. I figured on two hours for the entire job.

I pulled the rake lightly across the soil. It grabbed on a root and wouldn't budge. Hmm. I tried a different spot. Same result. I bent over and pulled at the root, a long, fibrous rope. It pulled up from the ground like a rip cord but had no end. I cut it off a few inches under the surface and tried another spot, but wherever I looked, there were roots, living roots, in the ground. All kinds of roots: endless, fibrous roots; bunches of deep roots from wild grasses that had to be removed with a pickax; long, lethal poison ivy runners. Christopher Walken had cut the weeds and shrubs off at the surface and left all their roots intact. I couldn't possibly plant grass in this soil in its present state. I spent the remainder of that day and all of the next yanking and digging at roots and sucking ibuprofen to ease the throbbing in my joints. Afterward, my body, not used to such physical labor, ached for days, and I seethed for weeks. Worst of all, though, was that my dream of having a gardener had rotted on the vine.

Christopher Walken soon faded into memory, but I had not heard the last of the blasted spikes. The following spring, I passed mowing responsibilities on to Zach, instructing him to mow with two wheels of the mower *inside* the edging. Finally we could cut the grass—all the grass—neatly with the mower, no weed wacking or hand trimming required. I had even bought a new Sears rotary mower to celebrate the occasion and replace the old, hard-to-start one. I unpacked the mower from the crate, gassed it up, and set Zach loose. Three minutes later, from inside the house I heard a horrible, indescribable sound, then silence. I ran outside. Zach was all right, just a little scared. He had hit something, that much was clear, but what? I didn't see anything on the lawn. I flipped over the mower, and there, in the housing, was a barely recognizable, twisted, mangled spike. I could see we were going to need a new mower blade. What I couldn't yet see was that the crankshaft had snapped and we were going to need a new mower. We had set a family record for destroying a new tool: three minutes. And my first thought was, *Walken!* But I walked through the garden and saw that a number of the spikes were protruding above the edging, a result most likely of frost heave. I guess I couldn't blame him for that. Now I conduct a spring ritual of walking through the garden with a mallet, checking and resetting all the spikes, before the first mowing of the season.

Zach was more or less permanently scarred from the experience. I still cannot get him to drop two wheels inside the edging. I think he would as soon drive the car down the street with two wheels on the curb. As a result, the grass always looks in need of trimming along the beds, defeating half the advantage of the edging.

Still, the edging was overall a good investment, and it was nice—if a bit unnerving at times—having a gardener, if only for a short while. There was something magical about watching the edging progress up the garden while I was away.

I still dream about having a gardener. My fantasy gardener is an English gentleman of a certain age who wears a proper straw hat and knows how to use a stirrup hoe. He doesn't need to know all the Latin names; he just needs to know the weeds from the plants and a pine tree from a fir. We will call each other "mister." He will know exactly what I want. And every week we shall have a cup of tea together while we consider the garden. Whenever there is a problem, he will know how to solve it.

And boy, was I about to have a problem. A very big problem.

Cereal Killer

It's not nice to fool Mother Nature.
—Chiffon margarine commercial, circa 1972

There's a serial killer in the garden," I announced one summer day.

"As in c-e-r-e-a-l?" Anne (I think) joked.

"Look out the window," I instructed grimly. This was no laughing matter.

I meant "serial" literally. Several days earlier, a single stalk of corn, the last plant in the last row, had toppled over during the night. I didn't think much of it at the time. It had been windy, corn is fragile—hey, stuff happens all the time, and besides, we had lots more. But the following day, when the *adjacent* stalk in the same row had toppled over, that seemed a bit strange. And the day after that, when the next adjacent stalk was toppled, bringing the total to three in a row, I remembered the words of a long-forgotten high school science teacher: "One event is an anomaly, two is a coincidence, and three a pattern." I had to admit, reluctantly, that it wasn't chance or wind at work here. But what was it?

On closer examination, I could see that each stalk had been eaten off neatly where the roots emerge from the stalk. I immediately suspected my old archnemesis, the groundhog. Had Superchuck returned? At this point I was blaming just about every family misfortune on groundhogs or deer. I couldn't get them out of my head. While snorkeling, I saw deer hoofprints on the ocean bottom. I had even tried to blame a groundhog for destroying our pool over the winter. The insurance adjuster was skeptical.

"Let me get this straight. Your contention is that a groundhog somehow got under the pool cover, ripped the vinyl liner six feet under the waterline, and got out of the pool alive."

I nodded. He stopped writing in his notepad to look me in the eye.

"You'd have a better case if there was a drowned groundhog in the pool."

"Can you come back tomorrow?"

My claim was denied. The adjuster left me with some advice: "Next time, spring for ceramic tile."

Still, the prime suspect in the Case of the Toppling Corn remained a groundhog. The first step was to check the fence. I hurried home from work and went through my all-too-familiar routine of checking all the wires, measuring the voltage, and looking for gaps. Everything seemed shipshape.

The following day, two more stalks—the next two in the row—were lying flat on the ground. This was incredible! Now as Anne and I looked out the window, the entire lower half of the row was toppled, the upper half untouched. What kind of groundhog eats in such a structured manner, plant by plant, up a row? And besides, this seemed to be happening overnight. Groundhogs are not nocturnal. Could it be a raccoon? Perhaps, but there was still the problem of the serial pattern of destruction, stalk by stalk, moving up the row. I wondered what would happen when whatever it was reached the end of the row. Would it turn around and start down the next row? I didn't want to find out, but I was baffled, utterly baffled. Could it be something in the soil? I dug around one of the fallen stalks but didn't see anything out of the ordinary. I put out the Havahartattack for the hell of it. Nothing. I considered staying up all night and trying to catch the intruder in the act. This wasn't as extreme as it sounds—in my agitation, I was barely sleeping anyway—but before pulling an all-nighter, I hit upon a better idea: hooking the camcorder up for overnight surveillance. I got out the recorder, which had been collecting dust ever since the kids had outgrown their—ahem—cute stage, and looked for a way to connect it to a motion detector so I could catch the offending critter on tape. I was also going to have to rig it to a light, or all the video would show was the darkness. I turned the camcorder around in my hands for a while, read the manual, and examined the recorder some more, thinking of Bridget's brother, Lars, trying to hook up the disc.

There have been precious few times that my vocation and avocation—director of technology by day, gentleman farmer by night—have crossed, and generally I try to keep it that way, as each role serves to make the other more tolerable. But this seemed like the time for some collaboration between the technician and the farmer. Alas, after a few minutes, I had to admit, the director of technology didn't have a clue how to rig up this camcorder. After watching a little of Katie's first-grade skit— I guess it *had* been a while since we had used it—I put the damn thing back on the shelf.

Meanwhile, the intruder continued to progress through the corn, like the steady march of an invading army. Anne thought it might be deer, but I attributed that opinion more to her growing animosity toward our hoofed neighbors than to scientific analysis. Ever since the deer had gotten into the garden and eaten a hundred dollars' worth of her newly planted flowers to the ground, her somewhat fatalistic attitude about the deer had changed dramatically. One day she almost lost her exemplary cool at work. Leaving the exam room, a patient had the bad timing to ask Anne how to keep deer out of her garden.

"Shoot 'em," Anne replied without thinking. (This from the woman who wouldn't have anything more than a BB gun in the house a few years earlier.)

The patient was quite taken aback by such a harsh answer from this gentle woman of healing.

"But what about fencing? How high does it—"

"Shoot 'em," the good doctor repeated, her voice rising. "Look, nothing keeps them out, not fences, not electricity, not dogs. You have to KILL THEM!"

The woman quickly fled the office, probably glad she wasn't asking advice about her elderly mother.

Whatever the culprit, this was maddening. I was sick of problems, having dealt with an unending stream of groundhog intrusions, thieving squirrels, drought, and, most difficult of all, serious lawn infestations for several years running. Of all these problems, the lawn infestations were the most irritating, because the lawn has always taken a backseat to the vegetable and flower gardens on our property. I am not a big lawn guy. As long as it's not too horribly weedy and brown, I let the landscaper cut it, and I ignore it. But lately, I couldn't.

When George was building the garden, I asked him to put sod around the swimming pool, which is down on the lower end of the yard. Having tried twice to start a lawn from seed in the horrible dirt and clay, I had decided to splurge and buy an instant lawn. Much to my surprise, however, I learned that sod takes quite a bit of care to get started—even more, in fact, than seed. The day George installed the sod, he took me aside like a football coach talking to his quarterback during a time-out.

"Make sure you give it two inches of water every day," he instructed me firmly.

Two inches? Isn't that a lot?

"Don't skimp," he warned, pointing at me for emphasis as he drove off. To keep the roots from drying out, sod needs copious amounts of water, much more than seed requires. And when your plot is as irregularly shaped as ours is, consisting of strips bordering a rectangular swimming pool, you either have to move the sprinkler repeatedly or water by hand. To sequentially give each strip two inches — even one inch — of water takes a good deal of time. Thus I found myself immersed in an unanticipated harried routine that went like this: rushing home from work to start the sprinkler on the first strip, climbing the 150 feet up to the house, eating dinner, going back down to position the sprinkler for the next section, coming back up the hill to the house, and going back down a couple of hours later to reposition it again. At a minimum. Usually, at least once an evening, the spike of the impulse sprinkler would work itself loose in the wet soil and start whipping wildly about the lawn like a crazed, spitting serpent, or it would become jammed and, instead of oscillating, remain fixed in one position until the sod threatened to float away. So night after night, I went up and down the hill, up and down, usually returning to the house wet, angry, and, by the end of the night, exhausted.

Even with all of this attention, the sod started to turn

brown at the "seams"—the edges where each twenty-four-inch strip of sod meets the next. Apparently I was skimping. Terrified at the specter of seeing my investment turn to dust, I redoubled my efforts, watering, watering, and watering some more, until somehow—after hours and hours of dragging hoses and sprinklers around, un-jamming and replanting sprinkler heads, and patting down the seams, the sod "took" and rewarded us with a beautiful, lush lawn.

For a while.

The following year, strips of it started turning brown, but not only at the seams, which were now pretty much all blended in. After looking in my lawn-disease reference book, which wasn't much help (every disease makes a lawn brown, but none looks exactly like *your* kind of brown), I dug up and carried a square foot of sod to my local garden center, where they instructed me to dig a few inches under the roots of the adjacent healthy sod and look for bugs. Their advice was sound: a few inches under the sod were small brown worms we identified as sod web-worms. I had never seen these creatures before and was now seeing them only in the sod—my one-year-old sod. Could they have arrived in the sod like so many tiny Trojan horses? It seemed unlikely, given the chemical nature of sod farms, but the evidence was somewhat damning. They were not in any other part of the lawn, and I had never had them until I imported the sod. It was also possible that they were partial to bluegrass, but I had been using bluegrass in a mixture for years without attracting the nasty critters. No, I figured they had most likely hitch-hiked in with the sod. That's what you get for buying a lawn instead of growing one. I gave the lawn a hefty dose of insecticide (which required yet more heavy watering), and the sod webworms were soon forgotten, but not before having done considerable damage to the new sod.

Having saved the lawn from webworms, I promptly proceeded to destroy it for good by planting four rosebushes.

I was new to rose gardening but instantly fell in love with roses. They are incredibly, almost indescribably, beautiful, a so-beautiful-it-hurts kind of beautiful. Roses seduce multiple senses: sight, smell (oh, the smell!), even touch. Not the roses you receive on Valentine's Day or see in most garden borders. Those modern hybrids are but a pale imitation of real roses. Most roses today have been bred to produce tight, whorled petals on long stems. Along the way, the rose's raison d'être, its very claim to our hearts, our literature, our culture—its scent—has been bred out, along with the dense layers of petals of varying blushes and hues. The roses I'm talking about—*real* roses—are sexy, powerful aphrodisiacs with pink and peach and pale yellow petals that suggest blushing Victorian maidens and sex in the bushes. These true roses can still be purchased today as "heirloom" roses, although I substitute a modern version of the heirloom that blooms a couple of times a season, the so-called English rose developed by David Austin, a British rose breeder.

Surely something this beautiful must come with a catch. I soon found out what that was after I had planted four of them in a border by our swimming pool. Just *four* of them, not forty or four hundred, yet these few roses would have a severe and permanent impact on my local ecology.

I can't say that nature didn't try to warn me. The earth resisted these shrubs mightily, the hard, dry clay finally yielding to repeated swings of a pickax. Each blow to the earth reverberated through my middle-aged body until, by the fourth hole, it felt as if the pick were driving into my spine instead of the earth.

That's when Zach came trudging by on his way home from school, bent under the weight of his backpack.

"What'ya doing, Dad?" he called as he approached.

"Just a little gardening, Zach. Planting some roses." Whap! I swung the pick into a clod of clay.

"That's not gardening, Dad," he said without missing a beat as he passed. "That's mining."

And so it feels sometimes. It must be wonderful to live on soil where one can actually dig a hole with a shovel. I know people do it, I've seen it in books, but it's a luxury I will probably never experience. Several times I considered quitting and giving the rosebushes away, but I persevered, and the next year we were rewarded with spectacular blooms, bursting with a heady perfume, painted in soft, undulating pastel tones. Oh, they were gorgeous, and classy! Even the names were classy. The Abraham Darby exploded into large blooms with various peach, salmon, and pink tones all appearing in the dozens of petals that made up each dense flower. And the smell! To some it suggests citrus; others detect peach or honey. I just call it heavenly. Graham Thomas offered various shades of soft yellow and a slightly spicy smell. I was so taken by these roses I even considered converting the entire kitchen garden to a rose garden, but my stomach directed otherwise.

As the roses bloomed, Anne displayed a domestic skill neither of us ever suspected she had: flower arranging. She started bringing large bouquets inside, arranging them with the lavender that grew beneath the rosebushes, and displaying them in vases throughout the house. Almost miraculously, the antique-looking roses elevated our old, slightly shabby interior to a respectible antique. Who knew that flowers held such power?

Our euphoria over the roses, however, was short lived. One June day, Katie saw a pretty bug sitting on one of the roses in the garden.

"Dad, is that a ladybug?" she asked. "It's pretty."

I wandered over.

This "ladybug" was four times the size of a ladybug, and it was *eating* the rose.

"That's no lady."

"What is it?"

I went up to the house to check my reference book. By the time I returned with the answer, Katie had found another dozen of them.

Japanese beetles. Remarkably, I had never even seen a Japanese beetle in my life. They are rather pretty (in the abstract), sporting a metallic copper shell that gleams in the sunshine, and I could see why Katie was attracted to them. I was going to have to deliver some bad news.

"We have to kill them," I told Katie. "Or we're not going to have any roses left."

Her face fell.

"Want to help?" I plucked one off the rose and crunched it between thumb and forefinger.

"Gross!" Katie exhaled and headed for the house.

Well, that was tactful. Couldn't I have just dropped it into a jar? Now I had lost my helper. And helpers—paid or otherwise—were in short supply. As gardens were spreading like purslane around the property, maintaining those gardens was becoming more and more of a challenge. In addition to the two-thousand-square-foot kitchen garden, there was a cottage garden Anne had created in front of the house; a hillside of lilies and lavender planted for erosion control; a spring bulb garden; separate beds outside the kitchen garden for mint and horseradish, two invasives that spread underground; and of course the rose garden. Any one of these secondary gardens was itself larger in size than all of our Yonkers landscaping combined. Anne helped when she could but had her hands full with the echinacea, black-eyed Susans, mullein, and foxglove in the cottage garden. We did, however, have two able-bodied kids whose contributions to the garden thus far were limited to consumption. One summer evening while we ate dinner on the porch, Anne tried to get me some help.

We were eating fresh corn off the grill, and the reviews from the kids were as shining as the corn itself, glistening under melted butter.

"Dad could really use some help with the garden," Anne ventured, sensing an opportunity.

"Not it," Zach quickly said.

"What about that actor?" Katie asked, apparently having overheard us discussing Christopher Walken.

"He went back to Hollywood," I said, not wanting to go into it with the kids.

"Did I miss something?" Zach asked, puzzled.

Anne pressed on. "You know where all this great food you love comes from, right?"

I think they did and they didn't. They knew, of course, that the food was coming from our garden, but they didn't really connect the time and toil that went into it with the food that was showing up on the table. It just kind of showed up, or at best, one of them was sent out to pluck a few sprigs of basil. While I wanted their help, I had to acknowledge that the kids had other chores, and the garden really was *my* hobby. Besides, I wanted any help to be voluntary, or at least given willingly. There is nothing worse than a cranky, unhappy kid in the garden—especially when it's someone other than me—so we didn't press the issue. They did both offer to help me out with nongardening tasks (thus giving me more time to garden), and I gratefully accepted (or fell on) that two-edged sword.

Back in the rose garden, I watched Katie climb the hill to the house, sighed, and picked the beetles off by hand. As with the tent caterpillars that had almost devastated the apple trees, by the following day, dozens of new beetles had arrived, and it was clear that I was in another death match.

Because we do bring roses into the house, and because we so treasure their perfume, I was reluctant to use a smelly insecticide on the bugs. So, following my usual progression of pest control, I picked and pinched for a few more days, but I was losing the battle—and the roses. I then moved on to an "organic" pesticide (pyrethrins, which kill on contact, but only if you "catch them in the act"), then to a stronger organic substance, rotenone, and finally, when that proved ineffective, to a manufactured chemical pesticide (containing carbaryl and malathion), which, if I had started with it in the first place, would have saved many roses and much aggravation.

Notice the progression of degree of contact with the insect as the battle escalates. First you start out with physical contact (pinching); then you move on to direct contact with a spray; finally you dispense with contact altogether and slather the bush in a chemical with a residual effect that kills the invader while you are in bed or at work. As with my apple-farming experience, I again found that, while I coveted the organic ideal, one of the problems with organic pest control is the degree of contact it requires with the invaders. Most of us hobbyist gardeners aren't around our plants enough hours of the day to become that intimate with the pests.

Eventually I did eliminate most of the beetles, and I only had to contend with the black spot fungus that English roses seem particularly susceptible to. But unbeknownst to me at the time, the battle had only just begun. The following year, all grass within fifty feet of the roses started turning brown in early summer.

Sod webworms again? I wasn't sure. These brown spots looked different, not like sod webworms at all, more like drought. I gave the lawn extra water, but the browned-out area continued to spread until it had taken over most of the lawn. As is my wont, I studied, analyzed, and pondered while the brown patches spread, until I finally remembered the advice I had received last time, to dig around where the diseased turf meets the healthy and look for insects. I put a spade into the brown turf, but it wasn't necessary; the turf could easily be peeled away from the roots like a zipper. I was shocked. No wonder the grass was brown—it wasn't attached to the roots! I scampered around the lawn on my knees, grabbing handfuls of turf that came out effortlessly. A little digging revealed a few small white grubs. *Oh, great,* I thought. *Yet another new pest.* I looked them up in the book and was dumbfounded to learn that they weren't a new pest at all, just a new form of an old pest. Grubs are the larvae form of Japanese beetles. Son of a bitch! I'd had no idea the two were related!

I had killed the beetles, but not before they had laid, I don't know, maybe millions of eggs in my lawn, and the larvae from these hatched eggs were now getting even, like the progeny of some science fiction alien. And soon *they* would metamorphose into new Japanese beetles, who would feed on my roses right above them, and *they* would lay millions of eggs in the lawn, which would hatch into grubs, and . . .

My head was spinning. What had I started here? I looked into an organic solution and learned about milky spore, an organism that you sprinkle from a can onto your lawn. It is harmless to most soil life but attacks grubs. The only problem was, it takes a year or two to become effective, and even then it is not always successful. Two years? I wasn't going to have a blade of grass left in two *weeks* if I didn't do something soon. Beetle traps were an option, too, but they have to be placed well upwind of the roses — that would be in Larry's yard — and it was way too late for that, anyway. I slathered the lawn in diazinon and repeated the treatment two weeks later, but the lawn was by now pockmarked with patches of bare dirt and toupees of loose brown grass. The sod, what was left of it, would never regain its former glory. And despite the chemical treatments, the following year would bring more Japanese beetles, and more grubs. Because of these mere four rosebushes, I now have to treat the lawn for grubs regularly. Fragile ecosystems indeed!

The common view (including, generally, mine) of chemical pesticides is that chemicals upset the natural balance of nature, while organic processes maintain the balance. Now, maybe I'm just trying to rationalize dosing my lawn in diazinon, but it does seem that in the case of my roses and beetles, the situation seemed to be quite the opposite. The natural balance was upset *organically* (by the introduction of roses), and it was the application of a pesticide that *restored* the prior condition. This is not to say that I advocate the wholesale application of pesticides. I am old enough to remember *Silent Spring*, and I remain a committed environmentalist, using pesticides reluctantly, guiltily, and only as a last resort. I'm sure that watering the lawn with diazinon did not come without a cost: in addition to the grubs, I probably killed every earthworm and beneficial bug in the top six inches of the soil. (In fact, diazinon, a derivative of nerve gas research from the world wars, has since been taken off the market because of concerns about its effect not only on fish and wildlife but on the workers who manufacture and apply it.) But the end result, at least, was that the pesticide restored my lawn to the grub-free condition it had been in before the introduction of the roses. An environmentalist would argue, correctly, that a lawn is not a "natural condition" to begin with. But I would add that neither are vegetable and rose gardens.

THE OLD BARN on the property is connected to the kitchen garden and the house via a wide, grassy lane, bordered by low stone walls, that we refer to as "the driveway," even though the last vehicles to drive down it were the two wrecked cars that we found in the barn when we bought the house. A month or two before the corn started toppling over like tenpins, sections of this driveway began to turn brown in parallel strips and odd rectangular patterns. I dug around, under, and near the brown spots but didn't find any bugs, so I turned to our landscaper for a diagnosis. Carmine — this was before he fired us — was thrilled at the opportunity, having just completed a course in the treatment of lawn diseases and being eager to put his new training to work. He pulled up a couple of blades of grass and held them up to the sky, turning and examining them while alternately pursing his lips and squinting. Then he consulted the reference book he kept in the truck and came up with a diagnosis: some fungus, I forget the name. Cure? Maybe none, but a pricey fungicide application *might* work. Oh, well, at least it wasn't insects this time. I did a little research of my own and found that, for this particular fungus, the most effective treatment was to keep the grass well watered and healthy. As we were in the midst of yet another drought, this was not easy. I tried, but the more I watered, the worse it got, and it seemed to be progressing up the driveway from the barn to the garden. Nevertheless I kept watering, like a good soldier, hoping for a turnaround that never came. By midsummer the grass driveway was shot through with brown stripes and rectangles, my Hudson Valley version of English crop circles.

And now the corn was toppling over, stalk by stalk. Plus another apple-thieving squirrel was in the orchard. Not to mention that after several blissful, bug-free years, Colorado potato beetles had finally discovered I was growing potatoes and had moved in for the kill. What next? Indeed what was *left*? Crop circles, toppling corn—things seemed to be spinning out of control.

I was useless at work, distracted and short tempered. What was I doing here? I should be at home, protecting my crops. Over the years, my colleagues had suffered my complaints about groundhogs and deer, endured my obsessions with Japanese beetles, and witnessed my stealing apple blossoms from hospital grounds. Now, trying to get my attention while I only wanted to talk about my corn, they must have wondered if I was going over the edge. Admittedly I was only going through the motions of working when a programmer came into my office for help with some computer code.

"The program just started blowing up all of a sudden," he said. "It was working yesterday."

"You haven't made any changes?"

"Nothing," he insisted. "Can you take a look?"

I had other things on my mind. Maybe if I just gave him some guidance, I thought, he'd leave my office so I could go back to pondering my garden problems.

"I'm a little tied up right now," I said. Which, in a sense, was true. "But consider this: the problem may be *appearing* here, but I suspect it was caused by a change you made somewhere else. You're too focused on this piece of code. Go back through all the modules you've changed in the past week. Somewhere you've introduced a bu—"

The word "bug" was hardly out of my mouth when I realized what I was saying. I needed to get another look at my garden. I checked my watch. Two o'clock. Close enough. I headed home.

Standing above the garden, I looked at the progression of brown stripes from the barn, up the driveway, to the garden gate, to . . . the corn. Of course. If the two problems were related, it could only be one thing. I grabbed a trowel and started digging in the corn bed, not under the fallen corn as I had a few days earlier, but under the adjacent, healthy corn. And there I found them—bugs. Sod webworms, merrily munching away on the corn roots. That was no fungus in the driveway; it was sod webworms. They had started at the pool, eaten their way up to the barn, then up the driveway into the garden, right up the grass paths in the garden, which Bridget had insisted on but I had never wanted and had let myself be talked into. Those . . .

those . . . those . . . I was apoplectic. Only one word would suffice . . . those FUCKING grass paths! Again! Arrrggh! I was beside myself. Panicked and giving hardly a second thought to the environmental or dietary implications of it, I immediately soaked the entire corn bed in enough diazinon to clear out every living thing in that bed. It was either stop the filthy critters now, or treat the entire garden—up to this point, a totally organic garden—later.

So there it was. I had done it. Somehow spraying apple trees had become acceptable—distasteful, but acceptable—and as I've said, I'd reconciled myself to the application of pesticides to restore the balance of the lawn, but soaking a vegetable-garden bed in diazinon represented for me a sad defeat, prompted as much by anger as by wisdom.

The evening that followed was oppressive, sticky and suffocating. The house fan droned through the night but was only replacing the hot, humid air in the house with the hot, humid air outside. I gave up trying to sleep around midnight and went downstairs, where it was a little cooler, then outside to look at the sky. I ended up in the garden, lying on my back as the gathering clouds obscured the stars, thinking about the garden, the universe, and the lessons I had just learned about both human nature and Mother Nature.

On the human side, neither the landscaper nor I had looked at the situation objectively. I was so primed from prior experience to look to an animal as the culprit, I had unconsciously closed my mind to other possibilities, no matter how obvious. The pattern of destruction, "like the march of an invading army," should have been a tip-off to look for an army. And the only place it could be was underground. As for Carmine, he had just attended a class on fungi, so he saw a fungus. If he had just taken a class on sunspots, I suppose he would have seen sunspot damage.

But as revealing about human nature as this episode was, the main lessons here are to be learned—as usual—from Mother Nature. I am always amazed (and a bit awed) at the chain of events in my miniature ecological landscape and the unexpected relationships between seemingly unconnected events. Plant a rose, lose a lawn. Buy a lawn, lose the corn. I had never seen either grubs or sod webworms, and now, because in one case I reached for ultimate beauty, and in the other, tried to buy an instant lawn, I may have to battle both for life. And this is but an infinitesimal example of the complicated webs that connect all living things. All I did was plant four rosebushes. What happens when we dam a river? Replace a hundred-acre field with a shopping mall? Do we even know enough about the complex environmental relationships to be *able* to do a so-called environmental-impact study? It's almost all too enormous and dizzying to even contemplate. As the sky clouded up, I thought about my corn, a staple of the Anasazi diet, and how easily I could have lost every last ear. I considered the disappearance of the Anasazi from the Jemez Mountains. Maybe it wasn't drought. Maybe they had planted something new—maybe even a flower—that attracted bugs that killed the corn that fed the Indians. It's a complicated business.

And I thought about the last time I lay in this very spot, before it was a garden, when Anne and I gazed at a starry sky, and how innocent and hopeful I was then. I yearned for a return to that innocence, to the perfect garden that existed in books and catalogs and our dreams. A drop of rain fell, making me laugh. *Is that the best you can do? Come on, bring it on, big guy. How about some thunder and lightning, just to make sure I got the message?* But I was denied even my dramatic denouement. It only drizzled, a few of nature's teardrops landing on my face.

Statuary Rape

*I would much rather have men ask why I have
no statue than why I have one.*
—Cato the Elder

Anne wanted an obelisk. For the center of the garden. Not just any old obelisk, but a six-foot, pink granite "Cleopatra wuz here" monument the local garden center had been trying to get rid of for two years. Think the Washington Monument with a small ball atop it. Without the windows. And pink.

Another test for our marriage.

It has been said that married couples should not be bridge or doubles-tennis partners. Some would add gardening partners to the list, and come to think about it, how often do you actually see a husband and wife in the garden together, working side by side? It can be like trying to grow mint and horseradish in the same bed. In our case, the garden ultimately brings us together more than it separates us, but sometimes it does become an alfresco boxing ring, complete with corner posts and (electric) ropes.

We went a few rounds one Saturday morning after I had missed a couple of weekends of hoeing. The cucumber bed was choked with purslane, the corn bed was a disaster, and the tomato plants were competing with chicory for their very survival. Looking out the kitchen window, I sighed. "Jeez, the garden's getting out of hand."

"Don't worry, I'm spending the entire morning in the garden," Anne assured me, having heard, I assumed, my cry for help. Relieved, I went out and did some errands, and when I returned in the afternoon, the cucumber bed was still choked with purslane, the corn bed was a disaster, and the tomato plants were competing with chicory for their very survival. Anne was dozing by the pool.

"I thought you were going to work in the garden today," I said, inadvertently waking her.

"Oh, hi," she yawned. "I did. Four hours' worth. Now I'm sleeping." She rolled over to one side, signaling her desire to end the conversation.

I wasn't done. "You sure you were in *our* garden? What did you do?"

She rolled back to face my sarcasm. "I deadheaded the cosmos and marigolds and tied up the asters."

Say what? I was incredulous. The garden was weedier than an abandoned lot, yet Anne chose to spend her four hours removing inconspicuous dead flower blossoms? I didn't want to start a fight, but I couldn't just let it go, either. This wasn't the first time this had happened. "I thought you were going to weed. The beds are a disaster."

"Oh, are they? I'll do them next weekend." She yawned again. She hadn't even *noticed* the weedy beds that were screaming at me every time I came within fifty feet.

"Next weekend! The garden will look like the Amazon by next weekend." For someone who didn't want to start a fight, I was hurtling down a weed-choked path of no return. "I don't understand it. How could you not notice the weeds? You do this all the time. You say you're going to help out in the garden, but you don't do the things I need help with. You just tend to your damn flowers." Uh-oh. I wished that hadn't slipped out.

Anne fumed, "I needed to work with the flowers today. Next week I'll weed." She rolled to her side, facing away from me, an alpha gorilla showing me her rump. Now the conversation really was over.

I was beaten. I tossed my towel and goggles angrily to the ground and headed up to the garden, where I attacked the weeds with a fury, misusing my shuffle hoe as an instrument of warfare rather than horticulture, separating the weeds from their life-giving roots with fierce "take that!" strokes. But in the serenity of the garden, surrounded by butterflies and bumblebees, I soon sweated out my fury, settling into my soothing shuffle-hoe rhythm, to and fro, slice and rake, reflecting on our fight. I came to understand that Anne saw nothing at all incongruous about her morning in the garden. Her goal that morning was a few hours of relaxation—deadheading, tying, cutting flowers for the house. My goal for the morning had nothing to do with the pleasures of gardening and everything to do with the often unrewarding but necessary *work* of gardening. Our agendas for the morning—which were not well communicated—were quite different. In fact our approaches to the garden in general are quite different.

I am goal driven in the garden. I head out there with a job to do, and I don't leave until it's finished. Anne heads to the garden when she *feels like gardening,* and unless I specifically direct her, she will spend the next few hours pursuing whatever activity brings her the most gratification. Now, there really is nothing intrinsically wrong with that; in fact, undoubtedly her attitude is far healthier than mine. She looks at the garden and sees the beauty and the peacefulness of it and disappears into the thick flowers, luxuriating in the sunshine. At those times, she becomes part of the garden herself, an animated garden statue. Sometimes, unseen, I watch her, her swimmer's shoulders rippling as she works the soil, beads of perspiration gathering on her forehead underneath a worn straw hat, her feet shod in red garden clogs. Occasionally she pauses to unselfconsciously perform a lovely, almost balletic maneuver, straightening up, arching her back, and wiping her brow. And I feel very lucky.

If she wants an obelisk, well, maybe I should just agree.

But six feet tall, and pink? And there was just something about it, something vaguely unsettling.

YET I'VE SEEN WORSE than garden obelisks. People do put strange things in their gardens, things much stranger. I confess I am not a big fan of ornaments and artwork in the garden. I don't mind a birdbath or a sundial, or even a Henry Moore, but I don't see where a glass gazing ball adds anything. And the thought of all that broken glass in the beds is unnerving.

Which might explain the popularity of plywood. There is a seemingly endless variety of plywood cutouts you can plant in your garden, from Huck Finn to howling coyotes to the classic bad-taste garden ornament of all time: a cutout of a stout woman bending over, revealing her bloomers. You might know the one, and admit it, you smiled the first time you saw it. And maybe the second. But surely not the third. I guess it's supposed to be cute, maybe even funny, but it just makes me cringe.

Some ornaments I find merely puzzling. A neighbor has a life-size ceramic deer in his yard. A deer! Excuse me, but in the Hudson Valley, putting a ceramic deer in your yard is like putting fake snow on the North Pole. What, there aren't enough of the real ones? Or could it be a kind of reverse decoy? Maybe the homeowner thinks this stud muffin with his twelve-point antlers will stake out the territory and intimidate the real ones into staying away. I'd be surprised if that worked, since dogs, loud noises, and pointing my finger and yelling, "Bang!" from ten feet away doesn't even cause them to flinch. Every time I pass by the house with the fake deer, I look over, hoping to see a real buck humping this dopey statue. I've noticed that you don't see many of these deer statues outside of town, in the rural areas. And if you do, they usually have bullet holes in them. Seriously.

Want a garden ornament that moves? You're in luck. Choose from a mind-boggling array of windmills, elves, whirligigs, and the poor woodsman who, prompted by the slightest breeze, chops at the same piece of wood eternally with his dull ax. These crafts are apparently created by people to whom miniature-golf courses represent haute architecture.

Perhaps you lean more toward the whimsical. Have you seen the statue of the rear end of a dog (the rest of it is burrowing in the ground)? How quaint.

No money to spend? No problem. Look around your garage. If Hudson Valley backyard artists can make garden sculpture out of discarded hubcaps, satellite dishes, and scrap sheet metal, you, too, can get that shabby-chic look without spending a dime.

When does a garden ornament become a garden structure? We found out while we were trying to sell our Yonkers house. I arrived home after a long day at the office to find a huge wooden structure looming over our postage stamp of a backyard. The neighbor whose backyard abutted ours had, in a single day while Anne and I had been at work, erected an enormous two-story pergola. Anne arrived a few minutes later and screamed. We felt as if we were living under a skyscraper. How on earth were we going to sell the house with that monstrosity, nearly as tall as our yard was deep, towering over us?

"You have to talk to him," Anne said. I get all the dirty jobs. "Be nice."

"I'm always nice." I winked as she rolled her eyes.

Oh, boy. I wasn't looking forward to this. I gathered my courage and walked around the block to explain the situation nicely to the neighbor, whom I knew casually, one of those suburban over-the-fence relationships where neither neighbor has ever seen the other one below the neck. He didn't say much that evening, and I left feeling my mission had failed, but to our surprise he disassembled the structure the next day, either because he was sympathetic to our plight, or perhaps because I seemed desperate enough to pursue the matter with the city, and he hadn't obtained a building permit.

Size, as they say, isn't everything. The most tasteless garden ornament I have ever seen is only a couple of feet tall. It is right here in town, in a neighbor's border garden. The house is on the route Anne and I take on our evening walks, and even in the dead of night, this stone object seems to absorb whatever moonlight or starlight is present and emit it back into the night with an eerie glow. We have walked by it hundreds of times, yet each time we pass, we still shake our heads in wonder and disbelief. Let me try to describe it.

It is a small statue, between two and three feet tall, light gray, which sits prominently among the pachysandra. The rough, textured stone is an aggregate, full of ocean pebbles, suggesting a sedimentary rock formed and shaped over billions of years of erosion, settling, compression, and wind (or alternatively, fifteen minutes in a cement mixer). The statue is crude, primitive in nature, vaguely reminiscent of an ancient Polynesian statue. In fact, it definitely looks like a primitive totem, an item of worship rather than one of decoration.

It is difficult to say whether its shape was formed by the forces of nature or a human hand. The stone rises erectly from the ground, the base a firm cylinder, or shaft, if you will, that flares out slightly near the top to form a bulbous cap, or head. This head is an elongated hemisphere (taller than it is wide) whose diameter is just slightly wider than that of the shaft on which it sits. In other words, the stone is a thick shaft with a rounded, flared head.

It is a stone phallus. A penis. Now, one might argue that this lovely piece of sculpture is really meant to evoke a mushroom, but let me tell you, I have seen plenty of mushrooms and plenty of mushroom garden ornaments (with and without the little leprechaun under the cap), and this is no mushroom. Anne, who ought to know, having seen (as a physician, I hasten to add) more penises than the Dallas Cowboy Cheerleaders, concurs: this is undoubtedly, unequivocally, unambiguously a penis, a totem penis.

What on earth is this thing doing in this man's garden? Has he seen one too many Fellini movies? It is such a weird object. I have visions of him coming out at midnight, kneeling before his totem, worshiping and making (who knows what kind of) a sacrifice. Spooky.

I can't figure out whether he's enjoying a small act of effrontery or is merely, like most gardeners, oblivious. Because we *are* oblivious. People—all people, including me—have no objectivity when it comes to their driving, their cooking, or their gardens. How else to explain stout ladies in bloomers, other than a total lack of objectivity about one's own garden?

THUS SURROUNDED BY the tacky, the tasteless, and the vulgar, I was determined to keep the pink obelisk out of my garden. I didn't need to give the neighbors any more reasons to be pointing at my garden and laughing. Not to mention the fact that we already had one phallic symbol in the neighborhood; I didn't want to be responsible for starting a trend.

We did have one ornament for a few years, a hefty, solid-brass sundial that even correctly told the time (but only two days of the year). Unable to find a suitable base on which to mount it, I had built a tripod base out of cedar fence posts, but I couldn't seem to secure the sundial to the base properly, so whenever a strong wind blew, the sundial blew off the tripod. Every time it happened, I was surprised. This was one hefty piece of metal, but the wind would get under it and flip it like a Frisbee. The kids thought the tripod looked, as they delicately put it, "stupid," so, tired of picking the sundial off the ground and defending the tripod to my family, I eventually took it down until I could find a decent pedestal. This turned out to be a mistake, because nature abhors a vacuum, and a certain piece of pink granite was ready to step in to fill it.

I found myself holding my breath and peering expectantly into the back of the station wagon every Saturday when Anne returned from her weekly shopping at the green market and garden center (conveniently located in the same location). Anne looked at the obelisk every week. I know she looked at it. But weeks went by, and the obelisk remained in the garden center, beckoning, biding its time. I think the expense of the object was holding her off as much as my disapproval. But then something strange and unexpected happened.

I started to kind of like it.

I began to see why Anne was attracted to it (without delving too deep into Freudian psychology). It had a beautiful texture, not polished, but not rough, either. Its smoothness somehow gave the unyielding stone a soft feel. And even on a hot summer day, it felt cool to the touch. I found myself walking by it whenever I was at the garden center, rubbing my hand on the stone knob at its top as I passed. It would certainly last a lifetime — several lifetimes — and would only improve with age and weathering. And perhaps if we ran our hands over the granite sphere each time we passed, it would eventually take on a soft, hand-rubbed patina, and generations from now, gardeners not yet born would run their hands over it and feel the wear from ours.

On the other hand, it was six feet tall, and pink.

But I told Anne we should think about it, and I could see the joy in her eyes. But no rush, I told her. It wasn't like it was going anywhere; it had been in the same spot for two years. And she agreed it *was* awfully expensive. So now price was really the only impediment holding us back. Thank goodness it was expensive. Then in October something else unexpected happened.

It went on sale.

The pink obelisk with the ball on top was marked down 40 percent. Anne was excited, but I still had my lingering doubts about the object. Forget my hand-rubbed patina — future generations will have plenty of other reminders of me; they'll still be picking my Kentucky bluegrass out of the tomato bed. But having opened the door a crack, I was having a hard time closing it. Anne seemed determined not to let this sale opportunity pass, and even I was thinking it was now or never. But still, there was just something about it, something that made me uneasy, something I wasn't able to put my finger on. But 40 percent off . . .

The obelisk was still on sale when we went for a family

drive in the country, looking for pumpkins. As we were driving, Anne said excitedly, "Oh, look, an obelisk." I looked over. Sure enough. A big obelisk. Cool. And there was another. And another. I'd never seen so many obelisks, big ones, little ones, gray ones, white ones! What was this wondrous place, this enchanted land of obelisks?

A voice from the backseat: "Dad, why are we driving to a cemetery?"

A little, muffled cry escaped from Anne's hand-covered mouth. It *was* a cemetery, and the obelisks were gravestones. Naïfs (okay, idiots) that we are, this came as a huge revelation to us both. So that's what the "something" was about it that I couldn't put my finger on, that association I couldn't quite place: it's funerary! Of course! How could we not know that? And just like that, the spell was broken, and the thought of a pink granite obelisk in the garden seemed as absurd to us as, well, a stone phallus.

Maybe I'll build a new tripod for the sundial.

Harvest Jam

For I have had too much
Of apple-picking: I am overtired
Of the great harvest I myself desired.
—Robert Frost, "After Apple-picking"

It was approaching midnight in the kitchen, and I could hardly keep my eyes open. After putting in full days at our jobs, Anne and I had turned the clock back to 1850 and spent the night canning peaches like all good homesteaders. Hours of nonstop peeling, slicing, packing. Peeling, slicing, packing. We wasted nothing: the overripe peaches went into peach sauce (delicious ladled warm over vanilla ice cream); the firm ones got canned. The way we salvaged every scrap, you'd think we were a family who *had* to live off the land, rather than a couple of professionals who were doing this for fun. At least, it used to be fun.

In past years, we looked forward to and enjoyed this annual event despite the hard work and resulting layer of sticky peach juice that covered everything in the kitchen,

including us. The ritual, apart from its appealing quaint-
ness, seemed in some way to validate our way of life and
the hard work that went into building the garden and orchard, and reinforced our philosophy of eating and buying locally. (And as the peach tree is ten steps from the
kitchen, you can't get any more local.) We developed a reliable and comforting routine over the years: an early dinner, get the kids to bed, slip some Joni Mitchell into the
CD player, and haul the equipment down from the attic.
Then, hours of canning while we worked, sang, flirted,
and sweated before falling into bed, sticky and exhausted.
That was then.

This particular year it felt more like a chore than a joy,
an evening of acting out a ritual that no longer held any
real meaning or purpose. Our main goal seemed to be to
use up the blasted peaches that were assaulting us with
their sheer number. We both kept sneaking glances at
the bushel basket, watching the level drop depressingly
slowly until we were out of jars and stamina—but not
peaches. I secretly suspected that, outside in the dark,
peaches were ripening faster than we were processing.

Unlike apples, peaches have a short shelf life, and
truly tree-ripened peaches (as opposed to peaches picked
rock hard for shipment to market) have a shelf life closer
to hours than to days. Thus there is an inevitable degree
of pressure associated with the harvesting and use of
them: there's no putting it off till next week. Once you've
made the pies, the cobblers, the fruit salads, and the

melba, there's nothing to do but preserve. And it *is* rather thrilling to be eating your own peaches in January as the snow falls, when summer is a distant memory. But this year the business of canning just seemed overwhelming, and as I stood in the kitchen sweating over the boiling water, I wondered what was different. Had I lost my interest in the ritual? If so, what did that imply, for gardening is largely about ritual, from the starting of seeds under fluorescent lights to the final turning over of the beds. Indeed it is the very ritual of gardening, the comfort of repeating something familiar year after year, that keeps many of us coming back every spring. I pondered that thought while Anne and I continued peeling, slicing, packing; peeling, slicing, packing. Something unspoken was hanging in the moist kitchen air, lingering like the smell of rotten fruit.

The bottomless bushel basket of peaches on the kitchen table started me thinking about the entire process of harvesting and storing and preserving. When I first started growing, I never gave it a thought. You grow things, you eat them. Or more accurately, you grow things, and the deer, groundhogs, beetles, and webworms eat them, and you eat what's left. But as I became a successful gardener, something almost unexpected was happening: I was producing food. Lots of it. As in two hundred pounds of apples. Bushels of peaches. Fifty pounds of potatoes. In a good year (and many were not), baskets of tomatoes, cucumbers, and leeks. Which meant that I was no longer "picking" fruits and vegetables; I was now, well, *harvesting*. I had become part of that ancient tradition of harvesting and storing.

The harvest holds a revered, even mystical, place in virtually every society on the planet. Even Americans whose hands have never touched soil observe Thanksgiving and sing "Shine On Harvest Moon," which celebrates the full moon nearest the autumnal equinox—the moon that lights up the fields for the season's final harvest. Although most of the ancient harvest rites have vanished, the tradition of the harvest festival still exists today, from Africa to Canada; it's a time of community celebration, of postharvest dances, parties, and weddings.

While harvesting for me is more of a family (if not solitary) affair, not a community one, I still feel the power and magic of the moment. We do have one small ritual of our own, Katie and I, when we harvest potatoes. By the end of summer, we have been "stealing" potatoes regularly, rummaging around in the soil to snatch a handful for dinner, but once the foliage has died off, it's time to collect the rest. I always call Katie out to the garden to help. After pitchforking most of them out of the ground, we dig through the soil with our bare hands, feeling blindly for the remainder, getting wonderfully dirty in the process. Katie excels at this job, for neither maturity nor strength offers an advantage. Without fail we play a game we first started when she was six. Katie declares there are no more potatoes to be found, and I tell her there's always one more, and to prove it we dig around some more until one of us comes up with another one. "Well, that's the last one for sure," Katie says. "Let's go inside." I say, "I'll bet you there's one more," because there's always one more, and we dig some more, and sure enough we find another one. I always make sure Katie finds the final one of the harvest.

She wants to be logical. "Dad, how can there always be one more? That's impossible."

"I don't know—there just is," I answer insufficiently. I want to be mystical. Things happen in the garden. "There's always one more" has become our code phrase, our shared secret knowledge between father and daughter, and we use it outside the garden as well, but sparingly, so as not to sap its power.

Rituals are as old as civilization. They provide comfort and safety. Insurance against tragedy. For as long as a child must dig the last potato of the season, kneeling beside her father, laughing "there's always one more," how could harm possibly come to her? The extinction of a life is tragic; the extinction of a ritual seems unthinkable, impossible.

Thus throughout the world, harvest *is* ritual. For the gentleman farmer or backyard gardener, it is something more, a feeling that is hard to describe. It is, to borrow an overused word, one of *empowerment*. Once I started harvesting, I was no longer a hunter-gatherer (at the local grocery store); I was now a farmer, providing food that I had raised from minuscule seeds for myself and my family. It's almost too much to grasp.

SOMETIMES THERE IS LITERALLY too much to grasp. Be careful what you wish for. The problem is, unless you are really disciplined at staggered planting (I'm not) and have a long-enough season for it (for most crops, I don't), when your crops come in, they come in more or less all at once. How many zucchini can you eat over a two-week period? How many cucumbers? When you can't consume all of it, you must store it, preserve it, or give it away.

We've always done a little of each. In addition to canning peaches, each summer we make enough sweet pickles and wineberry jam to last the entire year, with enough left over for wonderful Christmas presents. Recipients always appreciate receiving canned fruit and jam both because of the quality of it and because it is such a personalized gift. It is clearly something that you labored over. However, I've always been a bit self-conscious about giving away fresh produce because of a certain ambiguity that hangs in the air about whether it's the receiver or the giver who's doing the other the favor. To look at it another way, when does "giving" become "dumping"? Let's face it, when you have thirty pounds of zucchini hanging off your vines, each one doubling in size every twenty-four hours, giving a bagful to your neighbors is not exactly a moving show of generosity. And one is never sure what the neighbor is going to do with it. Have you ever been offered zucchini or a bag of tomatoes from someone who themselves received it from someone? I have, and always feel embarrassment for the anonymous gardener who doesn't suspect his merchandise is being passed around behind his back. Of course, when the gift is a bagful of juicy, ripe peaches or just-picked strawberries, one hopes that the quality of the fruit, not the abundance of it, is the message that comes across.

Never has this mixed message been better illustrated — or more awkwardly handled — than by my jogging partner, Scott, himself an avid gardener. For years, before I had a garden of my own, Scott subjected me to an uncomfortable weekly ritual, one that I imagine was repeated with other friends of his as well. It went like this: After each workout, Scott would offer me either zucchini or cucumbers from his garden. Then he would lead me into his kitchen, where he and his wife would start digging through the refrigerator, examining the week's vegetables. Each vegetable wore a small swatch of masking tape with what I presume was the date of harvest written on it. Scott or his wife would pull out a cuke, glance at the date, then sometimes put it back and sometimes drop it in my sack, after first ripping off the tape. I assumed for years that the purpose of this system was to ensure that guests got only fresh vegetables and (like McDonald's, which puts a little toy clock above the coffee warmer stating the time that

the coffee must be discarded) to guarantee that old vegetables were discarded, not eaten.

Silly me. Scott and his wife let the cat out of the bag
one evening when they started arguing — right in front of
me — over which cucumber to give me. As Scott was dropping one into the bag, his wife interrupted.

"Wait, not that one," she said in an alarmed voice.

Not that one? My ears pricked up. I peered over Scott's
shoulder. The cucumber was dated yesterday.

"I think we have another one."

"I don't think so," Scott insisted.

Another one? I don't think so? What on earth were they
talking about in this code? These were cucumbers, not
diamonds.

"No, I'm telling you," his wife insisted, getting angry.

Now I started to feel awkward. I was standing in their
kitchen after a hard workout, sweaty and smelly, and being
subjected to a marital argument over which cucumber —
retail value, approximately thirty cents — to give me.

She reached in and pulled out an older-dated cucumber, and then it dawned on me: the dates were part of a rotation system to ensure that cucumbers were used on a
first-in, first-out basis, the way your grocer moves the
freshest bread to the *back* of the shelf. Now, didn't *I* feel
special! I don't mind ShopRite's doing it, but I'd like to
think my jogging partner and longtime friend would give
me the freshest his garden had to offer, not the stalest.

Maybe I had misconstrued Scott's motives because I do

the opposite—to a fault—when giving crops away. When I bring apples into work, or give the neighbors peaches or tomatoes or strawberries, I want to put my best foot forward, so I end up giving away only unblemished fruit, leaving my poor family with the bottom of the barrel. As a consequence, we end up making a lot of applesauce while the neighbors are eating the good stuff. Admittedly this is kind of insane, but the alternatives—keeping everything or pawning flawed fruit off on neighbors—are not attractive, either.

Even an act as seemingly straightforward as bringing in garden roses for my office mates can send me on tiptoe through a minefield of social etiquette and office politics. Once, I brought in a couple of my English roses for a colleague who had done me a favor. She didn't have anything to put them in, so I fetched from my office a ceramic bud vase that Anne had given me years ago. A week went by, and the roses faded, and another week passed. Then a third went by, and the roses shriveled and turned brown but still remained in the vase. My vase. This raised two intriguing questions in my mind: Why was she keeping brown, shriveled roses on her desk, and was I ever going to get my vase—a prized gift from my wife—back? Did she think I was giving her the vase with the roses? After all, I was thanking her, but I wasn't *wooing* her. I needed a smooth way to get my vase back without embarrassing either of us.

I mentioned my dilemma over dinner.

"Why don't you go into her office," Zach suggested, "and say, 'My, look at those faded roses. Let me see if I can't do something for you,' and take the vase and dead roses out with you. She'll think you're coming back with fresh roses, and you get your vase back."

It worked like a charm, although it was not lost on either Zach or me that I was relying on my teenager for social advice. He had flipped the parent-child table on me yet again. But it was gratifying to see he possessed such social skills, much better than mine. This apple of mine seems to have fallen far from the tree.

Who would have thought that the act of giving could be so complicated? Yet it turns out that keeping produce is even harder.

The first couple of years that the apple trees bore fruit, we had nice, manageable crops that lasted us two or three weeks—joyous weeks of fresh, crisp apples eaten out of hand, fresh applesauce, and almost nightly pies, tarts, cobblers, and pandowdies. But as the orchard matured (and my use of insecticide grew bolder), my dream of bushels of apples came true—and with it came the realization that I hadn't given much thought to storage. A hundred pounds of apples is a lot of pandowdy. We had to come up with a way to store the apples.

When kept chilled and humid, apples can be stored in excellent condition for months. In fact, some apples, including the Grimes Golden that I grow, actually improve after a few weeks of chilling. But there was no room in our refrigerator for more than a couple of dozen apples. In previous years, I had experimented with natural cold storage in crawl spaces and the like. What I learned was that unless one has a deep root cellar (think *mine shaft*), this is a difficult proposition in the Hudson Valley. Empire apples, for example, ripen in late September, when it is still fairly warm—technically summer, in fact. Nevertheless I tried to store the apples naturally. This turned out to be an exhausting and unrewarding task.

At harvest time, the interior of our little barn was cooler than the outside air. In fact, a small room in the back corner of the barn was once used to store ice harvested from the Hudson River. The river was once home to a thriving ice industry, employing scores of men who cut through river ice with large handsaws and loaded the blocks onto horse-drawn wagons, to be taken through the valley into storage warehouses or private homes for use throughout the following year. Our "icehouse" is about five by eight feet, with six inches of sawdust insulation in the walls and a vent in the roof to allow excess moisture to escape.

It seemed like an excellent place to store apples. Perhaps it would have been had I first filled it with a couple of tons of Hudson River ice. As soon as the inevitable October warm spell hit, the temperature of the icehouse rose into the seventies, so I lugged all of the apples up the hill to a crawl space under the house, where it was cooler. The rats and mice and who knows what else really appreciated the unexpected delivery of these snacks, so a few weeks later when I discovered the damage, I moved what was left of the apples back to the barn, which had cooled down by then. This worked fine until the really cold weather came, and the unheated barn dropped below freezing. Frozen apples are no good. So back came the apples, 150 feet up the hill, a box at a time, now making their *fourth* trip between the barn and the house, where I stored them in a corner of the basement. Because of all of the exposed steam pipes snaking through the basement, it stays fairly toasty, but this corner was at least less toasty than the others.

By late December, I finally placed the source of the faint smell of cider that I had been noticing for a while. I retrieved the apples and threw out the worst of the worst, and Anne made applesauce with the rest. The net result of several months of moving apples from site to site like hot dice in a floating crap game was lots of mush and a few gallons of slightly musty-tasting applesauce.

Which is why the following year, with several bushels of apples hanging on our trees, I thought maybe it was time to splurge on a refrigerator to hold the harvest. We did a little looking around and found that it was going to cost close to five hundred dollars for a refrigerator large enough—eighteen cubic feet—to hold our annual crop. Now, granted, my apples are special. Though not organic by any stretch of the imagination, they are sprayed with far fewer (and less toxic) pesticides than commercial apples and, to my palate, taste far superior as well. I'm not sure I have ever tasted any apple finer than a Grimes Golden, with its perfect balance of sweet and tart, crispy and juicy. But is it worth spending five hundred dollars to have them through the winter? Not if you judge by market prices. We hemmed and hawed on the issue for weeks as harvest day drew near. Then when Anne pointed out that around Thanksgiving, when we typically entertain up to twenty-five family members, she often finds herself in need of an extra fridge, that cinched the deal. I didn't want to spend five hundred dollars to store a hundred dollars' worth of apples, but as long as we had another use for it . . .

We set the refrigerator up in the basement, turned the thermostat as low as it would go, and loaded it with apples stuffed into gallon bags that I had peppered with holes. Perforated bags seemed to provide a good compromise between holding moisture in and allowing enough out so that the apples don't rot. We filled the refrigerator to the brim. There were bags on the shelves, bags in the vegetable and fruit bins, bags on the door. Quite a sight. Opening the door was always a shock, no matter how many times I did it. But the biggest shock came when I realized that Thanksgiving was approaching, and the refrigerator was still packed to the gills with apples. Revelation time: apple harvest and Thanksgiving are both in the fall! There wouldn't be room in the refrigerator for a turkey or anything else on Thanksgiving. What on earth were we thinking? Had we confused Thanksgiving with Easter?

Looking back today, I don't regret buying the fridge, as

we eat fresh apples from our orchard into March of the following year.

For many winter-storage crops—potatoes, winter squash, onions—the moisture in the refrigerator would be as fatal as the warmth in the basement. These vegetables (okay, the squash, like the tomato, is botanically a fruit) prefer a cool, dry, and dark environment. Since Saharan caves are in short supply in the Hudson Valley, I didn't expect to have much success, but we've done surprisingly well storing potatoes and shallots—a member, like onions, of the genus *Allium*—in the basement, warm as it is. We hang the shallots in bunches and use them all winter long. Keeping another allium, the leek, through the winter is another story.

I love leeks. Not only do they make really great soup on a cold winter's night, but growing leeks makes me feel positively *medieval*. Unlike those New World discoveries potatoes and tomatoes, leeks are the stuff of monks and maidens. In fact, their cultivation goes back a millennium or two farther than that.

To keep leeks over the winter, you leave them right in the ground. They will not keep long in the refrigerator (or out of it), but will keep in the garden almost indefinitely if you can prevent the ground from freezing. So one late fall day, I tried the standard garden formula found in many garden books and covered the leek bed with twelve inches of straw, surrounded by a little fence of burlap that I made to keep the straw contained. When I was done, the bed had been transformed into a thick swath of yellow straw punctuated by the bulbous leek tops sticking through, waving in the wind like cheerleader pom-poms.

On a frigid mid-January evening, with a craving for a steaming bowl of leek soup, I trudged into the garden with a flashlight and a hand trowel, cleared away the straw from the base of one leek, and struck the earth with the trowel. Boingggg! The ground was frozen solid. I tried a couple of more spots: all frozen solid. Putting the hand trowel aside, I retrieved the spade from its winter hibernation and attacked the frozen earth. No go. It was like digging into granite. I didn't get the leeks out of the ground until a warm spell in February, when, in the kitchen, they thawed into a mushy, unappetizing mess. It was a total loss. "Twelve inches of straw will protect your soil from freezing," the book had said. Where? In Tallahassee? The book also neglected to mention that in the spring I would be faced with a massive cleanup job, as bits of straw had found their way into every nook and cranny of the garden. Even today, years later, I find bits of the stuff, an unwelcome reminder of the Year of the Frozen Leek.

I guess if I want to be harvesting leeks in January, I should really build a cold frame, which is like a mini-greenhouse. All you do is salvage an old window and build a wooden frame around it. Then just keep the glass free of snow, and you have a toasty little microclimate for cool-weather crops. It is said that with such a setup, one can grow crops like lettuce, leeks, and carrots almost twelve months of the year, even in the Northeast.

I have a large window I've been saving for years in the basement for such a purpose, but I just can't get myself to make the commitment. In the abstract, I love the idea of being able to eat my own greens twelve months out of the year, not just the five or six I manage now, but I'm not sure I want to be raising lettuce twelve months of the year. By October (if not months sooner), I'm all gardened out. I'm ready to put the damn beds to bed. And I don't think year-round gardening would be good for my psyche. I need some time to recharge, to be fallow myself, to review the successes and mistakes of the past year, and to make plans for the next. I need that time when the garden is quiet and the seed catalogs arrive and for a few months the garden becomes an abstract, a blank canvas, waiting quietly in anticipation of the new. The closest I want to be to my garden in January is opening a jar of peaches, hearing that satisfying pop when the vacuum seal is broken.

JANUARY PEACHES ARE SOWN in August. Thus on this long summer night, surrounded by pots of boiling water and steam, Anne and I continued canning peaches— peeling, slicing, packing. As the silence in the kitchen grew, I tried to understand what was happening. Neither of us wanted to say anything aloud, but after nearly twenty years of marriage, our nonverbal communication was often sufficient. Our lives were changing, catching up on us.

The solitary, noncommunity harvest had become the perfect metaphor for our lives. As we were becoming more self-sufficient in terms of food, we were simultaneously becoming more self-sufficient and insular in other ways. We had started spending holidays quietly at home instead of traveling to be with family or turning out huge dinners for twenty-five. We turned down invitations to parties. Stopped going to church. Just a month earlier, we had broken our "orphan rule"—our somewhat neurotic policy of never both getting on the same plane without the kids— for the first time and flown to Europe, just the two of us, realizing we no longer had forever.

Anne was exhausted, running herself into the ground, trying to meet the demands of a small-town physician in a solo practice, a dinosaur fighting extinction in a dawning era of group practices and medical corporations. And I was frustrated with Anne's exhaustion, missing her, and feeling frightened from the tingling I was starting to feel in my hand after working the hoe for a bit.

So the last thing either of us needed to be doing on this sweltry night was canning peaches for hours on end. More peaches than we could possibly use. We, like the trees, were groaning under the burden of plenty. But what to do with the bushels of peaches still on the tree? Another exhausting evening of canning was out of the question. But my ruminations on the meaning of harvest suggested an elegant solution. The next morning, after a couple of phone calls, I found to my surprise that not only was the local food pantry willing to take fresh, perishable fruit from a backyard orchard, but they were delighted to have it. I just had to pick it and bring it to the loading dock. I enlisted Zach's help and we worked side by side, filling box after box with peaches. It was the first time my son had ever been in the orchard with me, and though he didn't seem to be particularly enjoying himself, I wondered if I was creating a future fond memory for him.

The remaining harvest—a respectable ninety-nine pounds—was thus distributed throughout the Hudson Valley along with the usual fare of canned goods and corn flakes to (I'd like to think) some surprised and appreciative recipients. With that simple act, our harvest was transformed from a disagreeable burden to a rewarding, memorable gift. Anne and I didn't attend any harvest festivals or dances, but we had found a way to make our little harvest a bit of a community affair after all, and on that hot summer night, that was exactly what the doctor ordered.

The Existentialist in the Garden

Everyone gets the war they deserve.
—Jean-Paul Sartre

The image on the MRI was so clear, even I could make out what I was seeing. There was my spine, my vertebrae, and there, between the sixth and seventh vertebrae, was something dark oozing out on both sides, like a squeezed-down peanut butter sandwich. I had a herniated disc that was pressing on nerves on both the right and left sides of my spine. This explained the tingling down my arms, the weakness (the neurologist, a woman, easily beat me in an arm-wrestle), the chronically stiff neck. It wasn't life threatening, maybe not even terribly dramatic, but it *was* life changing. The next words out of the neurologist's mouth sent a chill down my herniated spine.

"No heavy lifting."

"For how long?" I asked.

She leaned in toward my face to make sure I understood. "This condition is not going away. Physical therapy

can relieve the symptoms, but your disc is not going to re-
tract back between your vertebrae. You have to learn to
live with this condition, and lifting is one of the worst
things you can do." Let me add some other things to that
list of worst things to do. Hoeing. Digging. Reaching high,
as in pruning. Pushing a lawn mower up a hill.

"So this is—"

"Forever."

Forever. And in an instant, I had morphed from a fifty-
year-old gardener to a seventy-five-year-old gardener. No
longer would I push wheelbarrows full of compost up the
hill; no tossing bales of peat moss over my shoulder. No, I
would have to garden quite literally like an old man, hiring people to do all the physical labor, maybe buying a
small tractor or golf cart to move heavy materials around
the yard. I would be reduced to puttering around the garden in a straw hat, like Don Corleone, picking tomatoes
and dispensing words of wisdom.

I felt a little dizzy. I wanted to scream. I wanted to cry.
I wanted to have an affair. I wanted to be young again.

"Continue the therapy, and I'll see you in three months."

Shit.

I have a theory of the origin of my herniated disc. Being tall, I'm predisposed to having neck and back problems to begin with, but when I graduated from high
school, what I wanted to do most in the world was play college (and in my fantasy, professional) football. I was an
impossibly skinny eighteen-year-old wide receiver, what

we called in those days a split end. Catch the ball and run like hell or, better yet, step out of bounds. The way I played it, football was *not*, for the most part, a contact sport. I was on offense only and was decent enough that I might have been able to play ball in college, except that the college I ended up at was Duke University—not a football powerhouse, but definitely a big-time football program. I showed up for summer practice in August as a walk-on, practically ignored by the coaching staff and other (scholarship) players, most of whom outweighed me by at least a hundred pounds, even the receivers. It was a brutal time. Picture North Carolina in August, three bruising practices a day (held, inexplicably, in a pasture full of fresh cow patties, although I never saw a cow), except on Sundays, when we were expected to show up at Duke Chapel (my first exposure to that weird relationship in the South between football and Christianity—don't get me started).

The tackling drills featured a technique that was new to me, one that is now outlawed in college football, called spearing. In high school, I had been taught to tackle a ball carrier by wrapping my arms around the player and putting a shoulder into his midsection, with my head off to the side. This is how tackling is taught today. But in 1971, spearing was all the rage, and the coaches at Duke and countless other colleges were instructing tacklers to lead with the head, sticking the head—not the shoulder—

directly into the ball carrier's chest, thus "spearing" the player.

Even to an eighteen-year-old, this sounded wacky and dangerous, not to mention ineffective. The coaches, aware of the potential for neck injuries, had added neck-strengthening exercises to the weight-room regimen. As if that could make any substantial difference overnight. Of course, I should point out that most of the defensive linemen had no discernible necks to begin with, although somewhere between the head and shoulders there was presumably a complete set of vertebrae.

Being a catch-the-ball-and-step-out-of-bounds receiver, I hoped I would be spared the spearing, but no such luck. Every player at Duke had to learn both an offensive and a defensive position, so in my alter ego as a defensive cornerback, I was subjected to long, agonizing drills every day, slamming my head and neck into a tackling dummy, *pow, pow, pow,* like a human pile driver. Occasionally I had to demonstrate the technique on a live body, although I was so inept at tackling that I usually missed the target altogether, to the mirth of my teammates and the ridicule of my coaches.

After a couple of weeks of three-a-days, I decided I had had enough. I was exhausted, dehydrated, and so far down on the depth chart I would have to fight the water boy for playing time. I clearly wasn't cut out for major college sports, so to the relief of everyone, I tearfully handed over my playbook and turned my attention to my studies. In 1976 the NCAA would outlaw spearing, but not before thirty athletes-turned-quadriplegics had traded in their football pads for wheelchairs. Today I can't help wondering if those weeks of pounding a skinny, still-growing eighteen-year-old neck into a tackling dummy set me up for problems more than thirty years later. Not that years of extreme gardening helped.

Regardless of the source, I had a new reality to deal with now. I had to reevaluate my place in the garden, the garden's place in my life. Actually I had already started that process even before (maybe in subconscious anticipation of?) the disc problems. The garden had sneakily been transforming itself from a place of solace and pleasure to, well, a pain in the neck. I had been trying to ignore this subtle transition the way a spouse ignores the obvious signs of a troubled marriage, but given my new physical limitations, it was time to face facts. I had a troubled garden, and I had to get it under control.

But what exactly was the trouble? Certainly the garden was too large for a fifty-year-old with a bad neck, and my stubborn resistance to mulch and plastic had ensured that it was always in need of weeding. All right, so Larry was right: it *was* going to be a lot of weeding. But something more was troubling me, more than having to mow the grass, than having to weed constantly. The garden no longer felt like *me*.

It is a pretty, and in most years productive, garden, the

kind of kitchen garden you see in garden magazines (except with lots more flowers), neat, linear rows delineated with grass and gravel paths. The rectangular beds are just the right size, and the drip irrigation makes watering a snap. Each year the soil grows richer with the addition of manure and compost. This is a *damn* good garden. So what was my problem? Why was I growing increasingly dissatisfied with it? What was wrong with those neat, linear rows? Those boring, neat, linear rows. Predictable, boring, neat, linear rows. It occurred to me that if I showed someone a plan of half the garden, he could, never having seen it, pretty accurately fill in the other half. But was my complaint really about symmetry? No, it was more than that. This garden was too linear, neat, and predictable, too—as I had said to Bridget all those years ago—Cartesian.

Sitting in the garden, staring out at these rows, I realized that, in the way we get the leaders we deserve, in the way that dogs often resemble their owners, I guess in the end we get the gardens we deserve. The French existentialist Jean-Paul Sartre said it another way: each of us gets the war we deserve. I wanted a garden that was sloppy, rambling, surprising, spontaneous. But I had to face it: as much as I hate to admit it, I am khaki, deliberate, and straightforward. Maybe that's what Bridget saw in me, and that's the garden she designed for me.

On this day, though, I wasn't feeling khaki and deliberate. Maybe it was the impact of seeing the MRI, the hint of mortality that it implies, the fact that I'd recently turned fifty, but on this day I felt—or *wanted* to feel—a little wild, adventurous, and unconventional. I wanted to live in Paris. I wanted to learn the guitar. I wanted to rip up these rows and replace them with rambling paths that disappear around a bend, under an arbor, that end up— where?

My biggest fear was that I would end up doing nothing. Several times over the past couple of years, I had wanted to make changes to the garden, only to find myself frozen by indecision until the urge passed. But doing nothing was not an option this time. The disc oozing from between my vertebrae had seen to that. Something needed to change in my garden, in my life.

The garden was less often satisfying these days. I still felt passionate about it, but now the passion I sometimes felt was *homicide.* But love it, hate it, or somewhere in the middle, I have never lost the passion, and I have always felt responsible. Responsible for its past, and responsible for its future. Design too linear? Grass paths? They're my responsibility, not Bridget's. Sod webworms in the corn? Grubs in the lawn? My fault. I installed sod, I planted roses. No tomatoes this year? Guess I did something wrong. When not agonizing over what to do with the garden *next* season, I feel weighed down by the choices I made *last* season, burdened by the freedom of choice, seared with passion, determined to squeeze the maximum out of its very existence.

In short, I am the Existentialist in the Garden. Camus in the chamomile. Sartre in the salad. How on earth did I get here, and how do I get out? Do I *want* to get out? If I leave, where do I go? If this garden is my war, then the golf course is surely Armageddon. What I've been doing is rewarding, nourishing, and reflective of a philosophical belief in self-sustenance and healthy, fresh food—but how do I make it *fun* again? This is, after all, supposed to be a hobby, not a burden. I think about the burden of canning peaches: my lesson in how quickly novelty becomes ritual becomes chore.

The great, terrifying existentialist question: If you were doomed to live the same life over and over again for eternity, would you choose the life you are living now? The question is interesting enough, but I've always thought the point of asking it is really the unspoken, potentially devastating follow-up question. That is, if the answer is no, then why *are* you living the life you are living now? *Stop making excuses, and do something about it.* A thorough examination of this issue is probably a quick path into therapy for most of us, but as the Existentialist in the Garden, I *have* been implicitly asking this question of my garden. Is this the garden I would build again? If not, why not? And what, if anything, should I do about it?

It's remarkable what's happened to this garden over the years. When Anne and I first contemplated building it, it was just a garden. This cigar really was just a cigar. Not a (conscious) extension of our personalities, or a political statement, or even an attempt at self-sustenance. It was a large, pretty kitchen garden, something we'd always dreamed of in the abstract. And to Anne, it largely still is. But when did it become something more to me, an inseparable part of me, a third partner in our marriage? More startling, why did it take me so long to realize how it had moved into our lives? After all, for years we'd been arranging vacations around harvests, I'd been spending virtually all of my leisure time between May and October tending it, and more than once it had sown marital discord.

Suddenly, given the limitations on my activity, the question was, How do I proceed? How do I make this work for me? Am I really ready to become Vito Corleone? I would have to think about that later. In a few weeks the first apples would be ripe. But before that, I would have to harvest the remaining peppers, potatoes, and tomatoes. There was so much to do.

The $64 Tomato

*We will gladly send the management a jar of
our wife's green-tomato pickle from last summer's
crop—dark green, spicy, delicious, costlier than
pearls when you consider the overhead.*

—E. B. White

Summer, like my tomatoes, was showing its cracks. A pre-back-to-school hush filled the school yards. The late-August nights were delightfully cooler, the days noticeably shorter, the afternoon shadows more angular. I watched a single rust-colored leaf blow across the garden the other day, a startling reminder of the passage of seasons, a hint of the winter to come.

But I still had tomatoes. Sweet, juicy heirloom tomatoes. I was in the garden, having just picked one of the few remaining Brandywines, when Anne came by and exclaimed, "What a beautiful tomato!"

"It should be," I joked lamely. "It probably cost us twenty dollars."

Anne looked at me, waiting for an explanation.

"We hardly got any," I said. "And we spent a lot on the garden this year."

"Surely you're exaggerating," Anne insisted, used to my hyperbole. I conceded that twenty dollars for one tomato was probably a gross exaggeration. But the exchange got me thinking.

Most of the gardeners I know don't garden to save money on groceries, although that might have been the norm a hundred years ago, when the backyard vegetable patch was a staple of most American homes. Most gardeners today garden because they enjoy the activity, or crave the freshness, or want vegetables, such as Brandywine tomatoes, that cannot be bought at the local Piggly Wiggly. Nevertheless it is reasonable to assume that it is cheaper to grow your own food than to buy it. That $1.79 pack of tomato seeds has the potential to feed a small community; most of us will use a half dozen of the seeds and throw out the rest, or use them next year. And the rest of the materials are free. You stir a little home-brewed compost into the vegetable bed, throw the seeds in the ground, add a little water, and presto, in a few months you have tomatoes, *n'est-ce pas?* Your initial $1.79 investment can return, I don't know, potentially fifty, a hundred, maybe even two hundred dollars' worth of tomatoes. Try to get a return like that on Wall Street.

But that isn't the total fiscal picture. I ran into a few expenses along the way before and after the ground was ready to receive those tomato seeds. Like building a garden. Like keeping the groundhogs and deer from eating everything in sight. This year seemed especially bad. I knew I had put a lot into the garden this year and hadn't taken an awful lot out. So just for the heck of it, I decided I would try to figure out just what this "free" tomato really cost.

I started with the costs of building the garden (orchard excluded):

Garden design	$300
Initial construction	$8,500
Extra charge for stump pulling	$300
Irrigation and drip hoses	$1,100
Cedar edging	$400
Electric fencing equipment (exclusive of charger)	$400
Posthole digger	$50
Posts for fencing	$50
Two wrought iron gates and posts	$400
Additional topsoil	$250
Havahart trap	$65
Velcro tomato wraps	$5
Cedar for tomato posts	$10
Steel edging	$1,200
Labor for installation of edging	$600
Forsythia border (including labor)	$700
Gas-powered hedge trimmer for forsythia	$75
Wood-chip mulch for forsythia	$300
Chipper/shredder for shredding leaves for compost	$400

Dark bark mulch (fifty bags at $3 per bag)	$150
Push lawn mower for lawn paths	$80
Bag for lawn mower (never used)	$40
Gas-powered lawn mower for garden	$215
Garden books	$100
Garden-magazine subscriptions	$150
Peat moss and other miscellaneous soil additives	$125
Removal of two trees	$600

Not counting thousands of dollars of my labor thrown in for free, or yearly expenditures on seeds and seedlings, I ended up with the shocking figure of $16,565. When Anne and I started the project, we put what seemed to be a generous limit of $10,000 on it, and true to the Rule of Thirty-two (any home project will take three times as long to complete and cost twice as much as planned), we ended up overbudget by 65 percent.

Of course, in doing my tomato valuation, I couldn't charge this all off against one year of gardening (only filthy-rich corporations with good tax lawyers could get away with that). Instead I amortized the cost of the garden over twenty years, by which time I would either be gardening somewhere else, not gardening, or rebuilding this garden. So to get the annual portion of the construction costs, I divided $16,565 by twenty years, yielding $828 per year. To this I added any additional expenses I incurred this year. As I have some expenses every year, I did not amortize them but charged them fully against this year's "profits":

New electric fence charger and supplies	$300
Mulch	$150
Adjustable garden rake	$15
Seeds and seed potatoes	$120
Hedge trimmer	$80
Replacement gravel	$20
Green-manure seed mix	$50
TOTAL	**$735**

Holy smokes! I spent another $735 on the garden this year without even realizing it! These costs plus this year's share of the one-time construction costs totaled $1,563. Now, since I was interested in the price of my tomato, I did not count everything that came out of the garden equally. I'm not even sure how one would do that. Instead I subtracted from the $1,563 the true market value (using the higher local farm-stand prices, not supermarket prices) of all the produce I harvested *excluding Brandywine tomatoes*. In the spirit of full disclosure, I should point out that this year was a terrible year for gardening (for me, anyway). We had record-setting high temperatures in July and August that decimated the lettuces and tomatoes, and I hadn't grown corn this year, further reducing my total yield. I don't usually weigh my vegetables (except potatoes, for some reason) as I bring them in from the garden, but judging by how many meals we got from our crops and how many jars of pickles we made, I was pretty well able to reconstruct the amount. But to be safe, I erred on the high side. Here is our yield:

Potatoes	$45
Lettuce and mesclun	$48
Squash	$15
Cucumbers	$15
Basil and other herbs	$35
Sweet peppers	$3
Sugar snap peas	$30
Green beans	$25
Cherry tomatoes	$20
Leeks	$48
Dona tomatoes	$10
Strawberries	$50

Representing $344 worth of produce, excluding Brandywine tomatoes. Now, $344 isn't exactly peanuts, but "gentleman farmer"? "Self-sufficient?" Who am I kidding? Three hundred forty-four dollars' worth seems like barely enough food to nourish the groundhog, let alone a family of four. In my meager defense, let me point out again that it was a very poor year (although, mysteriously, the local farm reported a great season); in other years we might be higher, but for this year we were stuck with $344. The other thing this reveals is that food is *cheap*. I actually grew a fair amount of food; it just wasn't worth much. For example, my local green market is selling a ten-pound bag of white potatoes for $1.50—just 15¢ a pound. A person could probably eat well from that buck-fifty bag for several days. (For this exercise I valued my Yukon

Gold and fingerling potatoes at $1.50 per pound.) Every time I'm done picking sugar snap peas or rise from my stoop, aching, from picking green beans, I marvel that I can buy this stuff in the green market for a dollar a pound. How can anyone possibly grow green beans for a dollar a pound? I can't even *pick* them for a dollar a pound, it takes so long. It's a miracle that any farmer stays in business, but God bless them.

Back to my expensive tomatoes. Three hundred forty-four dollars (the value of this year's yield) subtracted from $1,563 left a cost of $1,219 for my stash of Brandywines. How many did I get this year? At the risk of making too many excuses, I'll point out that the heat just shut down my tomato plants in August. It is a known fact that heat *before* blossom set will shut down tomatoes, but I'd always thought that August heat was good for tomatoes. When I asked Doris at the farm if their tomato crop was as meager as mine, she looked at me as if I were crazy. They'd had a great tomato year, but they grow Big Boy and Roma tomatoes; perhaps these varieties withstand heat better than my purebred heirlooms. Or maybe the fact that they mulch heavily kept the roots cooler and the plants more productive. Or maybe they're just better farmers than I am. After all, they've been doing it for generations.

I know, I'm stalling. So just how many tomatoes did I get this year? Exactly nineteen. The groundhog got almost as many. They were large and delicious, these nineteen Brandywines, and that number does represent a tomato a day for almost three weeks. Still, it doesn't seem like much. It *isn't* much.

Time, finally, to do the depressing math: $1,219 divided by nineteen equals—gulp—$64 per tomato.

Holy cow.

This was sobering. I never realized how much growing my own food was *costing* me. I went to Anne with the numbers.

"You won't believe this," I said. "Remember that joke I made about the expensive tomato?"

"Uh-huh," she said, distracted, as she leafed through the *New England Journal of Medicine.*

"Twenty dollars turned out to be a tad low. That was a *sixty-four*-dollar tomato."

"Maybe that one you stuffed with crabmeat? That was good," she said, not looking up.

"You don't understand. I'm not talking dinner-menu prices. Every Brandywine tomato we picked this year literally cost us *sixty-four dollars* to grow."

Now I had her attention. She put the journal down and stared at me for what seemed an eternity.

"And just how do you know that?" she finally inquired hesitantly, not sure she really wanted to know.

I laid the spreadsheet in front of her. She studied it for a minute.

"We spent all this on the garden?"

"Maybe more. I'm sure I forgot some things."

She pushed away the paper as if it were contagious and

flipped a page in her journal. "Well, we see this," she said, borrowing a phrase she often uses with patients. Meaning, in this case, that she was over the shock and ready to move on. And inviting me to join her. Truthfully I wished I hadn't done this exercise in accounting. Some things you're better off not knowing. I've said that the garden had become a family member, but at the moment it felt, not like the beloved grandmother you care for, but like the embarrassing uncle you avoid at weddings, loud and extravagant beyond his means, always in trouble, always in debt.

We see this. I, too, wanted to move on, but there was still one unspoken question troubling me, one that spanned months, years, ages. A question I both had to ask and was afraid to ask.

"Was it worth it?"

Anne deliberately closed the journal, placed both hands on the cover, and looked up at me.

And smiled.

Childbirth. Da Vinci. Potatoes.

I want death to find me planting my cabbages.
—Michel Eyquem de Montaigne (1533–1592)

I am sitting here, in late September, at my kitchen table, cradling a ripe, heart-size Brandywine tomato in the palm of my hand. A scarce few minutes ago, it was on the vine, a living, growing organism. Now it has brought the warmth of the September noon sun into my chilly kitchen, warming my hand, almost pulsing with life. In a few moments it will be lunch, but I am in no rush to slice into this lovely fruit, the last tomato of the season.

I will miss the fresh tomatoes, the crickety sounds of summer, the lobster rolls eaten on the porch. But I am also relieved that summer is over. Gardening is often thought to be a genteel, relaxing hobby, an activity for the women of the garden club as they dally about in their straw hats, fitting lotioned hands into goatskin gloves, sipping tea under the shade of a magnolia. I am not a member of that club. For me, gardening more often resembles blood sport, a never-ending battle with the weather, insects, deer, groundhogs, weeds, edgy gardeners, incompetent contractors, and the limitations of my own middle-aged body. And it turns out to be a very expensive sport.

So why do I persist? I can offer a few reasons.

First and foremost, I do it for the food. Some years ago, for better or worse, I crossed the line from gardener to family farmer, but truthfully, as long as I've gardened I've been motivated by the food. There really is nothing like a fresh August tomato. The leeks I grow taste more or less like the leeks from the supermarket; ditto the peppers and rhubarb. But a homegrown, vine-ripened tomato is probably more different from the store version than any other crop you can grow. I start salivating in June for a bacon, lettuce, and tomato sandwich made from a freshly picked, sun-warmed tomato. (Unfortunately I usually have to wait until August.) The food from your garden really does taste better. If you have a garden, you know what I'm talking about. If you don't have a garden, find a few square feet and grow even just one or two tomato plants. And make it worthwhile: Grow an heirloom variety such as Brandywine or Cherokee. If you're going to grow Supersonic or Big Boy, you might as well buy them from the farm stand. If you have more room, grow leafy lettuces and greens, including some arugula. And sugar snap peas. You may be astounded by what you taste.

But of course, I don't garden only for the food. If that were the case, I'd have done away with beds and paths a long time ago and switched to a small tractor in a field. And now, one can buy baby spinach and fresh mesclun mix at the grocery store year-round. Our green market even sells fingerling potatoes. There's clearly another imperative or two at work here.

Gardening is, by its very nature, an expression of the triumph of optimism over experience. No matter how bad this year was, there's always next year. Experience doesn't count. Just because the carrots have been knobby, misshapen, and somewhat bitter *four years in a row* doesn't mean they're going to be knobby and misshapen next year. No, sir, next year you will (1) work in twice as much compost and peat; (2) plant a new, improved variety; or (3) get lucky. Or even better, you can forget carrots and plant something exotic like blue cauliflower in that bed. Because every year starts with a clean slate, and the phenomenon I call garden amnesia ensures eternal hope. Even the cursed purslane weeds, being annuals, will die off during the winter, so as long as I didn't let any purslane flowers form and go to seed, I will at least be starting off with purslane-free beds. And next year I'll cultivate every week, instead of letting it go for two months. A mere ten minutes a week is all it will take, and . . .

Blessedly, the voice of experience, the voice that should be crying, "Oh, puh-lease!" never pipes up in the garden. And I, for one, hope it never does. It is not wanted there.

I also find myself fascinated with the cycle of birth and

resurrection in the garden. It surely is no accident that the Old Testament places the origins of humanity in a garden. Who can deny that his or her heart quickens at the sight of the first seedlings of spring peeking out from under the soil? First, there is the sense of wonder (and relief) each time a seed sprouts, a feeling of, "Wow, I did it! I guess I didn't plant the seeds too deep/shallow/close together/far apart/dry/wet/early/late." Then, to watch the miraculous: one tiny seed becoming, with the addition of nothing but dirt and water, a twenty-foot cucumber vine, bushels of tomatoes, thirty-pound watermelons; seeds no larger than a speck of dust—a speck of dust!—turning into tender, bright green lettuces. It doesn't matter how many years of biology I've studied or how many genomes scientists decode: to me it's still a miracle—incomprehensible, fantastic, and immensely rewarding. A human sperm and egg becoming a fifty-year-old gardener, now *that* I can somehow understand. But how these seeds become tomatoes and cucumbers and lettuce, it's all too fantastic and strange to fathom.

The perennials provide as much joy and surprise as the seedlings. Because of garden amnesia, every winter I hold the thin strands of what is undoubtedly dead clematis between my fingers and wonder what to plant in its place. And every spring, lo and behold, after everything else is green and vibrant and my clematis is still brown and dead, a day comes when I notice a couple of green shoots at the base, and a few weeks later the resurrection is complete and the plant is in full bloom, sporting glorious, broad, star-shaped flowers that wave in the slightest breeze.

And I tell Anne it's not dead after all, and Anne says, "You say that every year," and I say, "But this year it really looked dead." This, too, is part of the cycle of life and rebirth and hope and comfort in the garden.

One of my garden routines is to keep a garden journal, really just a few hastily written notes about each year's successes and failures, and reminders for next year. But the most significant piece of information I keep is the last frost date of each spring. This is a significant date, for most seedlings can only be put outdoors after all danger of frost is passed. I use this historical data to estimate the average last frost date for my garden, rather than rely on the Cornell Cooperative Extension's more general estimate for the county. Of course both the CE's date and mine are averages, not guarantees.

I still get a kick every year out of Katie's reaction when I tell her we have to plant some certain seed one week before the last frost date ("Dad, that's ridiculous. That's like saying, 'Take the popcorn out just before the last kernel pops'"), and I do get a small death-defying thrill (although the daring is tempered a bit by the fact that it's the seedlings' lives at stake, not mine) out of getting a jump on the season by gambling that the last frost will occur earlier than the cooperative extension's forecast. If I put the plants I've raised from seed outdoors before the "official" date, and there is no more frost, I am rewarded with earlier crops; if I've guessed wrong, I lose all the plants and have to (shudder) resort to buying replacements from the garden center. A silly game? Maybe. So other people habitually play lotto; I annually gamble with my grow-light-raised seedlings. I think I do it because it keeps me closer to the cycle, the cycle of rebirth and renewal. And because I'm dying for fresh lettuce.

I am also, I have to admit, a sucker for slick copy writing and beautiful photographs, experience notwithstanding. When the Burpee catalog's editorial board sits down to entice the American consumer with this year's "largest, sweetest [fill in the blank] ever, with jasmine-scented rose-colored flesh," they must have my picture on the wall with the caption "This is your target." They surely have my demographic, my income, my *gullibility*, down to a tee. I suppose it's not much of a challenge. Whatever they can come up with, not only will I buy it, but I'll pay extra for it. Garden books showing the world's great gardens similarly seduce me with dreams of re-creating that very same Victorian grandeur in my rocky, clayey backyard. What I forget—every time—is that great Victorian gardens came equipped with great Victorian garden*ers*, full-time staff with nothing else to do but clip and trim all week and start over again the next week. Because I have repeatedly failed to learn this lesson, I am (to cite just one example of many) saddled with a rampaging stand of creeping thyme in what used to be a patio area because I saw a lovely bluestone patio with creeping thyme growing between the stones in a "great gardens" book and thought, *I just have to have that in my garden. That looks so cool.* And indeed it did, for a few months, until the thyme, not satisfied with remaining a half inch high in the cracks, started to branch out—literally. The great garden's gardener must cut the stuff back every two weeks, a detail the author neglected to mention, and a schedule to which I am not able to adhere. At first I managed to clip it twice a season or so, then once a season; then I decided—well, not really decided, it just kind of happened—to let it go au naturel, and the former patio is now a very strange-looking patch of thyme, which, if you scrape underneath, reveals its bluestone origins like an archaeological dig. It does smell great when you mow it, however.

A common bumper sticker reads "A bad day fishing beats a good day at work." Yes, I've had some rocky times, but I suppose on most days, when the weeds are somewhat under control, the groundhogs tamed, and my neck isn't throbbing, I feel the same way about gardening. I remember an early-April morning some years ago, a day that I took off from work to plant potatoes. (May I suggest that this is a fine way to spend a day away from work.) It was the perfect day for a spring planting, maybe the first warm day of spring after a bitter, hard winter. It being a weekday, the neighborhood was empty and silent, no cars or voices. I spent the morning working compost and peat moss into the black soil, fluffy and warm and smelling deliciously of the earth. I luxuriated in the feel of the warm earth in my hands, a warmth and a smell that seemed to go right into my bones. I raked the soil smooth and cut trenches with a hoe as surprised earthworms scattered. I held one as it squiggled in the unfamiliar texture of my cupped hand. What a marvelous, mysterious symbiosis nature has created. The earthworms pass the soil through their digestive tracts, leaving a product more enriched and nutritious than what came in. At the same time, they break up and aerate the soil, their tiny tunnels creating an ideal environment for vegetables. This worm was long and fat; he was apparently finding my soil, now loaded with horse manure and peat, to his liking. I wondered where he had come from, how he'd gotten there. Did he burrow in underground from the backyard, occasionally poking his head up to see if he was under a stone path or a bed? Or perhaps he just took the sod webworms' Highway 61, that blasted grass that runs up the center of the garden. Either way, he had to somehow crawl from the grass to the potato bed. Did he climb over the five-inch cedar, or burrow underneath? And now that he was here, would he stay? Was this now his bed for life? How long would he live? Would he procreate?

I must have spent minutes with this wiggling worm before I set him down and watched him scurry off. Then, on my hands and knees, with my face only inches from the earth, I laid the seed potatoes in their new homes, five to a row, and covered them gently with soil. Halfway down the bed, I stopped, sat back on my haunches, and tilted my face up to the warm sun, eyes closed.

I was startled at the sound of my own voice, speaking aloud. "This is perfect," I heard myself say.

Things I remember: Witnessing childbirth. Finding myself standing absolutely alone before Da Vinci's *Last Supper*. And planting potatoes on a perfect spring morning.

The Ghost of Gardening Future was not standing over my shoulder that morning to tell me that in eight weeks, Colorado potato beetles would decimate the crop while I slept, and flea beetles would eat what they left behind. Nor did I know that my fingerling potatoes would refuse to grow, ending up the size of peanuts that year. No, at this moment my garden was the Garden of Eden *before* the fall, when everything was pure and beautiful, and I was blissful in my ignorance. Sometimes gardening is just plain *good*.

I'm not sure where the garden and I are headed, as we near the start of our second decade together. I have lots of questions but as yet no answers. But it seems to me that if we are going to stay together—and it's in both our interests to do so—we need to come to an understanding, this garden and I. For my part, I need to accept the garden for what it is—not the garden that I fancy someone like me *should* have—and it needs to be more tolerant of my limitations, particularly as I start sliding down the far end of middle age. Which may mean reductions in size, ambition, and perhaps even beauty. Which in turn means that I may need to decide just what kind of garden it's going to be: it's a difficult demand, asking a garden to be both efficient *and* beautiful. But isn't that what men have always wanted: the cook in the kitchen and the whore in the bedroom? *The whore in the bedroom and the horticulturist in the garden.*

I've been guilty of imposing the Madonna/whore complex on my garden, asking it to be both whore and horticulture. Seduce me *and* feed me. It has taken me nearly ten years to figure this out. But having acquired this insight, what now do I do with it? If I have to choose, which do I give up, the aesthetic or the stomach, the whore or the horticulture? I can eliminate many of my gardening woes with a few simple changes: erect a seven-foot chain-link fence; eliminate the grass; put plastic weed block in the beds. No, that clearly won't do. Flower gardens are easier. Give up the vegetables and grow flowers? And live without fresh tomatoes and baby greens? We may as well move back to the city.

The whore in the bedroom and the horticulturist in the garden. Too much to ask? I ponder this thought as I pick up the tomato again. I'm going to have lunch now.

ACKNOWLEDGMENTS

Were it not for my literary agent, Laurie Abkemeier, this book might never have seen its way into your hands. For that, and for her sharp red pencil; for bailing me out of more literary jams than I care to enumerate; and for introducing me to the wise and patient Amy Gash (who knows just how much rope to give a writer) and the superb Algonquin team, I am deeply grateful.

SUGGESTED READING

There are thousands of books on gardening. Here are a handful that come off my bookshelf most often.

Brickell, Christopher, ed. *The American Horticultural Society Encyclopedia of Gardening*. New York: Dorling Kindersley, 1993. Every gardener should have a ten-pound no-nonsense gardening reference book. This is mine.

Browning, Frank. *Apples*. New York: North Point Press, 1998. Browning's obsession with apples takes him from New York to Washington to Kazakhstan. A must-read for any home orchardist.

Hirsch, David. *The Moosewood Restaurant Kitchen Garden: Creative Gardening for the Adventurous Cook*. New York: Simon & Schuster, 1992. A surprisingly useful quick-reference guide to growing sixty-five vegetables and herbs, with some garden-design tips and a few recipes thrown in.

Otto, Stella. *The Backyard Orchardist*. Maple City, MI: Otto-Graphics, 1993. This is usually the first book I turn to when I need practical information on tending my fruit trees.

Pollan, Michael. *The Botany of Desire: A Plant's-Eye View of the World*. New York: Random House, 2001. For the truth about Johnny Appleseed, as well as some provocative thoughts on plant survival strategies and how those Idaho spuds end up on your table.

————. *Second Nature: A Gardener's Education.* New York: Atlantic Monthly Press, 1991. An alternate view of a life in the garden.

Reich, Lee. *Weedless Gardening.* New York: Workman, 2001. A perhaps overly optimistic, but original approach to fighting weeds from a Hudson Valley gardener and writer.

Robertson, Adele Crockett. *The Orchard: A Memoir.* New York: Metropolitan Books, 1995. A moving account of a woman's struggle to save her family's New England apple farm during the Depression.

Recipes

Oddly enough (okay, *understandably* enough), only a few readers have asked me for advice on, say, growing tomatoes or keeping groundhogs out of the pea patch (although many have *offered* advice). But I have frequently been asked for recipes for the dishes that appear in cameos throughout the book. So as a bonus to this paperback edition, and because it's easier than answering my mail, I've included them here.

I'll leave it to the reader to decide whether I'm a better cook than gardener. Bon appétit!

Leek Potato Soup

This is a remarkably comforting soup on a cold winter day (and gives you a good excuse to be in the garden while the home team is blowing a close one). With a loaf of fresh bread it becomes a meal. In the spring, substitute fresh asparagus or peas for the leek and you have two more reasons to cook soup.

Serves 4

3 to 6 leeks (about 1½ pounds before trimming)
2 tablespoons unsalted butter
3 medium potatoes, preferably Yukon Gold
4 cups low-salt chicken broth
½ cup heavy cream
salt and pepper to taste

1. Cut off and discard the roots and green tops of the leeks, leaving about an inch of green. (If using those large grocery store leeks, you will only need 3; if using garden leeks, more like 5 or 6.) Discard the outer one or two tough leaves. Slice the leeks down the middle lengthwise and clean well under running water, then slice into about ½-inch pieces. Save a small piece for garnish.

2. Melt the butter in a soup pot and sauté the leeks over medium heat for about 10 minutes, until they start to soften and turn translucent.

3. Meanwhile, peel and cut the potatoes into chunks. Add the potatoes and a box of low-salt chicken broth (yes, home-made is always better, but who's got the time?) to the leeks.

Bring to a low boil, then turn down and simmer with the lid ajar for about 30 minutes, stirring occasionally, until the leeks are tender and the potatoes are soft. Slice the reserved piece of leek into thin slivers and set aside.

4. Remove the pot from the stove and use an immersion (stick) blender to thoroughly puree the mixture. If you have only a standing blender, transfer the soup in batches until it is all pureed. You will probably go out and buy an immersion blender soon afterward.

5. After blending, return the soup to the stove and whisk in the cream. Stir more or less continuously until a simmer is just reached, then remove from heat and check the seasoning. Add salt and pepper to taste. Ladle into bowls, add the leek garnish, and serve.

Caprese Pasta

If our kids ever decide (despite witnessing my travails) to grow their own tomatoes, it will be because of this dish—their all-time favorite, made with fresh tomatoes, basil, and mozzarella. *Caprese* refers to the Italian isle of Capri, in the Bay of Naples. This is a pasta variation of the famous Caprese salad, which is made with tomato, mozzarella, and basil. The recipe takes only 25 minutes to prepare because you don't need to peel or otherwise fuss with the tomatoes.

Serves 4

> 30 fresh basil leaves, washed
> 1 pound medium shells or other pasta
> 4 or 5 heirloom or other vine-ripened tomatoes, about 2 pounds
> 8 ounces fresh mozzarella cheese
> 1 cup grated Pecorino Romano cheese
> 1 clove garlic
> ¼ cup extra-virgin olive oil
> 2 tablespoons chopped parsley (optional)
> Salt and pepper to taste

1. Go out to the garden or farmstand and pick 4 or 5 of the ripest good-size tomatoes you can find and about 30 leaves of basil. If you have parsley, grab a few sprigs.

2. Start a large pot of boiling, salted water. Slice each tomato in half across the equator and, over the sink, scoop out most of the seeds with your fingers. Don't worry about getting all of

the seeds out. Chop the tomatoes to medium dice and place in a colander for a couple of minutes to drain the excess liquid. Transfer the tomatoes to a bowl. Chop the basil and parsley.

3. Cook the pasta. We use medium shells for this dish, because they hold the thin sauce nicely. While the pasta is cooking, slice the mozzarella into ⅜-inch cubes. Grate the Pecorino Romano cheese.

4. Smash a clove of garlic with the heel of your hand and sauté very gently in ¼ cup of extra-virgin olive oil over low heat. Take care not to brown the garlic. Remove the garlic after a few minutes and add the warm oil to the tomatoes. Add the chopped basil and toss.

5. When your pasta is almost cooked, season tomatoes with a generous pinch or two of kosher salt and fresh ground pepper. (If you add the salt too soon, the tomatoes will render too much juice.)

6. When the pasta is cooked al dente, drain quickly (do not rinse) and return to pot, off the heat. Add the tomato mixture and the mozzarella. Mix in well and cover tightly. Let sit for 5 minutes, then stir again. The heat of the pasta should have partially melted the mozzarella. Spoon into pasta bowls. Sprinkle the parsley and half of the Pecorino Romano over top and serve with the remainder of the Romano.

Windowpane Pasta

(Adapted from the Williams-Sonoma *Complete Pasta Cookbook*, Chuck Williams, ed.)

Need an antidote to so-called "30-minute gourmet" cooking? This visually stunning but nearly two-hour project should do the trick. The original recipe calls for nasturtium butter (butter blended with finely chopped nasturtium flowers and a dash of honey), but we much prefer the thyme and lemon butter sauce described below.

Serves 4

For the pasta:
   3 large eggs
   2 cups all-purpose flour
   1 cup herbs and edible flowers

For the sauce:
   1 stick (4 oz.) unsalted butter
   2 tablespoons fresh thyme leaves
   zest of 1 lemon
   ½ cup freshly grated Parmesan or Pecorino
      Romano cheese

Make the pasta:

   1. Go into the garden and collect a cup or so of flat, small-leafed herbs and edible flowers: basil, parsley, sage, dill, chervil, nasturtium, violas. For the thyme sauce you will need enough thyme sprigs to yield about two tablespoons of leaves.

2. Prepare a basic egg pasta. We use our KitchenAid stand mixer outfitted with a dough hook, but you can use anything from your hands to a food processor. If using a mixer, briefly beat the eggs in the bowl. Add the flour, a little at a time, blending after each addition, until all the flour has been added. Increase the mixer speed to moderately high and continue kneading the dough for 5 or 6 minutes. If the dough is too moist, add a little flour; if too dry, another bit of egg. If too sticky, knead another minute or two. Finish with kneading a few minutes by hand on a floured countertop or board. When kneaded, the dough should have a pleasant, firm feel with a slight sheen. Keep the dough covered with plastic wrap during the next steps so it doesn't dry out (if it does, simply refresh with a dab of egg).

3. Set the rollers of the pasta machine at their widest opening. Pull off an egg-size piece of the dough, flatten it with your hand and run it through the machine. Fold it in half and run it through again. Do this a total 4 or 5 times, folding in a different direction each time. (You are completing the kneading of the dough.) Then adjust the rollers to the next setting and run the dough through (do not fold). Close the rollers one more notch and run the pasta through again, continuing this process until you've reached the narrowest setting on the machine or the dough is tearing.

4. Lay the pasta strip onto a floured surface and trim lengthwise into a 3-inch-wide strip. Return the excess to the ball of dough. Now cut your strip in half crosswise so you end up with two equal strips. On one, haphazardly arrange the

herbs and, if you like, the occasional small flower. You can pack them fairly densely, as they will move apart when you run the dough through the machine again.

5. Lay the other half strip over the first and press gently to seal. Adjust your pasta machine to the narrowest setting that will accommodate this sandwich (this may take a little trial and error), and run the dough through. Go to the next narrowest setting and continue as before. The herbs should be clearly visible through the pasta.

6. Set aside the strip on a floured surface and continue with the remaining dough.

7. Cut the pasta into 2-inch squares with a serrated pastry cutter or a knife.

8. Bring a large pot of salted water to boil and warm a large plate or shallow bowl in the oven.

While the pasta is drying and your water is coming to a boil, make the sauce:

1. Gently melt the butter into a 10- or 12-inch sauté pan. Keep warm.

2. Strip the leaves off of the fresh thyme by drawing thumb and forefinger down the stem, against the grain, until you have about 2 tablespoons.

3. Remove the zest from the lemon.

Now it's time to put it all together:

1. When the water has come to a rolling boil, gently add the pasta squares, stirring so that they do not stick together or to the bottom, about 2 minutes. You may want to do this in two batches. (*Do not overcook:* fresh pasta cooks *much* more quickly than dried!) Note that you will need to save a bit of the cooking water for the sauce.

2. Turn the heat up under your butter to medium high. When the foam subsides, add 3 or 4 tablespoons of the pasta cooking water and whisk vigorously to make an emulsion. Whisk in the thyme and lemon zest and remove from heat.

3. Add the drained pasta and some freshly ground pepper to the sauté pan, tossing gently for one minute. Arrange on a platter, topping with freshly grated Parmesan or Pecorino Romano cheese. Garnish with nasturtium and violas. Serve with additional grated cheese.

Potato Apple Thyme Gratin

Some dishes taste great for the first bite or so (ginger ice cream comes immediately to mind), but grow tiresome thereafter. Others, like this unusual gratin of potatoes and apples, start slowly, but the subtle taste of this dish grows more appealing with every forkful. The apples release a good deal of juice, imparting a mild sweetness to the potatoes.

Serves 4

2 large Yukon Gold potatoes (about ¾ pound)
2 large apples (about ¾ pound), cored and peeled
1 medium onion, sliced
1 tablespoon fresh thyme leaves
5 tablespoons unsalted butter
salt and pepper to taste
⅓ cup dry white wine
⅓ cup water
1 tablespoon sugar
⅓ cup freshly grated Parmesan or Pecorino
  Romano cheese

1. Peel and slice the potatoes, apples, and onion into ⅛- to ³⁄₁₆-inch slices. Strip the leaves off several sprigs of thyme until you have about a tablespoon.

2. Heat 2 tablespoons of butter in a medium frying pan and gently sauté the onion and thyme with a generous dash of salt and a few twists of pepper until the onions are translucent, about 10 minutes. Do not brown.

3. Add the wine, turn up the heat, and cook for a couple of minutes until the wine is reduced by half. Add ⅓ cup water, another 3 tablespoons of butter, and the sugar. Cook, stirring until the butter is melted, and set aside.

4. Alternate layers of potatoes and apples in a buttered gratin dish, adding some of the onion mixture between layers, finishing with a layer of potatoes. Bake, covered with foil, for 45 to 55 minutes at 375°F until the potatoes are tender. Remove foil and sprinkle the top with the grated cheese. Return to oven for another 15 minutes or so until cheese begins to brown. Let sit 5 or 10 minutes before serving.

Aunt Teh's Bread-and-Butter Pickles

This recipe for sweet pickles is from my sister-in-law's Aunt Teh (which makes her my . . . uh . . . who knows). We've never used any other. The first attempt at canning can be intimidating. You have to keep everything sterile; you have to buy Mason jars, rings, lids, and a large pot for sterilizing. But if you stick with it, pickling can be among the most rewarding things you'll ever do with your harvest. Note that pickles are much easier to can than peaches. This recipe will yield about six quarts of fantastic, crisp sweet pickles to eat with sandwiches year-round. They'll keep in the pantry for months, but chill before serving.

Note: This recipe is not a lesson on canning. If you've never canned before, please read a canning book before proceeding so that you're familiar with the aforementioned intimidating sterilization and canning techniques.

25 to 30 six-inch cucumbers
6 to 8 large onions
2 red peppers
½ cup kosher salt
5 cups apple cider vinegar
5 cups sugar
2 tablespoon mustard seeds
½ teaspoon cloves
1 teaspoon turmeric

1. Slice the cucumbers (we plant a small variety specifically intended for pickling) and onions on a mandoline or V slicer to about ⅛-inch thick. Slice the peppers into thin strips.

Combine the cucumbers, onions, and peppers with the salt, let sit at room temperature for 3 hours, and drain well. The salt will draw out a quite a bit of liquid.

2. Combine the remaining ingredients in a large kettle and bring to a boil. Turn down heat, and add drained cucumbers and heat thoroughly, until steaming. Do not let boil.

3. Meanwhile, sterilize your jars, rings, and lids. We sterilize the jars slightly ahead of time and keep the rings and lids in a saucepan of simmering (not boiling) water until we're ready for them. Ladle the hot pickles into sterilized quart Mason jars, packing in as many as you can fit. Then ladle in liquid to within ¼-inch from the top. Clean the top of the jar with a sterile cloth, top with a lid and twist on a ring. Immediately turn the jar upside down and place to the side. After 5 minutes or so, you can turn the jars right side up and wait for each lid to pop, indicating that you have a good seal.

Anne's Applesauce

This is a great way to use up less-than-optimal apples. Anne makes hers far less sugary than the commercial variety, allowing the taste of the fresh apples to come through. An old-fashioned food mill is ideal for making applesauce, as it allows you to eliminate the step of having to core and peel the apples. Cooking the apples with the skins on gives the applesauce a beautiful color, and the skins and seeds are later filtered out by the food mill.

7 or 8 Empire or Macintosh apples (about 3 pounds)
1½ cups water
2 tablespoons brown sugar
1 teaspoon cinnamon

1. Core and quarter the apples.

2. Place in a saucepan with the water, brown sugar, and cinnamon. Bring to a boil, then simmer, covered, about 20 minutes, until the apples are soft.

3. Run through a food mill and serve warm.

Anne's Peach Pie

Fresh peaches tend to be quite a bit juicier than grocery store peaches. Some of the juice will end up spilling over, so put a foil-lined cookie sheet on the shelf below the pie to catch the drips.

For the pie crust:

  2¼ cups unbleached flour
  1 teaspoon salt
  2 teaspoons sugar
  2 sticks (8 ounces) cold, unsalted butter

For the filling:

  8 peaches (3 to 3½ pounds)
  1 tablespoon lemon juice
  1 cup sugar
  2 tablespoons of unbleached flour
  ⅛ teaspoon salt
  ⅛ teaspoon ground nutmeg
  1 tablespoon unsalted butter
  2 tablespoons sugar

Prepare dough for two crusts:

  1. Combine 2¼ cups of flour, 1 teaspoon salt, and 2 teaspoons sugar in a food processor and pulse briefly to mix.

2. Add 2 sticks of cold unsalted butter, cut into tablespoons, and pulse until the mixture is the consistency of coarse meal or small peas.

3. Remove dough and sprinkle in about 6 tablespoons of ice water, more if necessary, until you can form the dough into a ball. Press into a small disk, wrap in plastic, and refrigerate while you prepare the filling.

Make the filling:

1. Peel the peaches by scoring the skin all the way around with a sharp knife and dipping into boiling water for a minute, then into ice water, one or two at a time. (Alternatively, use a serrated vegetable peeler.)

2. Slice the peaches into a bowl and toss with the lemon juice. In a separate bowl combine 1 cup sugar, 2 tablespoons flour, and a dash (⅛ teaspoon) each of salt and nutmeg. Add this mixture to the peaches and toss until evenly blended.

Assemble the pie:

1. Halve the dough and return one half to the refrigerator. Roll out the other half into a 10-inch round, enough to cover your pie plate and the edges. Use the roller to transfer the dough to the pie plate.

2. With a slotted spoon, add the peaches, leaving excess juice behind, and dot with 1 tablespoon of butter.

3. Roll out and add the top crust, pressing the edges with your fingers. Trim off excess dough and make several vent slits in the top crust with a sharp knife. Sprinkle 2 tablespoons sugar over the crust.

4. Bake in a 450°F oven for 10 minutes, then reduce heat to 350°F and bake another 30 minutes or until top is golden brown. Allow to cool somewhat before serving.

WILLIAM ALEXANDER has been gardening and small-scale farming for over twenty-five years. He is a contributor to the *New York Times* op-ed page, where he has opined on such varied issues as the fundamental differences between leaf rakers and blowers and the difficulties of being organic. He lives with his wife and their two children in New York's Hudson Valley. *The $64 Tomato,* a Quill Award Finalist, is his first book.